Unders
Cryptocurrency

Three Guides to Using and Profiting From Digital Currencies

Collecting:
Understanding Bitcoin
Ethereum: A Primer
And
Cryptocurrency: A Primer

By

Eric Morse

Table of Contents

Understanding Bitcoin

Ethereum: A Primer

Cryptocurrency: A Primer

Understanding Bitcoin

A Beginner's Guide To Cryptocurrency

By

Eric Morse

To the early adopters, who learned all of this the hard way so that others wouldn't have to.

Introduction

Bitcoin is quite popular lately, and rightfully so. This new technology provides people the world over with an alternative way to shop, save, invest, and transact outside of the traditional financial infrastructure. In the Philippines, for example, when one of the country's biggest banks went offline for two days in June of 2017, millions were unable to pay their bills and daily expenses. But a few had already embraced Bitcoin and were able to pay for many of the things they needed those two days. In 2010, traditional payment processors (Visa, MasterCard and Paypal) stopped doing business with Wikileaks, completely disabling that organization's ability to collect donations. Enter: Bitcoin. Wikileaks funded itself almost exclusively through Bitcoin for some time, and Bitcoin still has a prominent place on their donations page.

In this book, you'll learn what Bitcoin is and how to use it securely to pay for goods and services. I'll also touch on using Bitcoin as an alternative form of investment, and how to invest should you decide to do so. By the end, you'll be in a good position to start using Bitcoin for practical and investment purposes.

This book assumes that you have not read any of my previous works on cryptocurrency. Out of necessity, it will cover some of the same ground as **Bitcoin: A Simple Introduction**, which focused on presenting the basics of Bitcoin in the most simple way possible. That book shied away from certain topics (mining and investing, for example) that I didn't see as suitable for an intro-level primer. With only a few exceptions it also didn't name specific websites, software or businesses. Those blinders are removed for this book. **Understanding Bitcoin** is intended for the slightly more advanced beginner, if there is such a thing. It is for people who want to know *"Where To Go"* and *"What To Do,"* whereas **A Simple Introduction** is more focused on *"What is This Bitcoin Thing I Keep Hearing About?"*.

Some things to know up front:

Things change rapidly on the internet and change even faster in the world of Bitcoin. If you are reading this book years after I've written it (in early 2017) the companies and websites I discuss in this book may have gone out of business or significantly changed their areas or methods of operation.

Also, the Bitcoin ecosystem is large and growing. Since this book is not a directory of Bitcoin businesses, I cannot list every business, website, hardware vendor, etc. I chose to list those that are the most well-known or that I have had personal experience with in the past. If I do not mention a specific business or website, it should not be taken as a warning, negative opinion, or statement of disapproval. With the exception of links to my other books, I have not included any affiliate links in this text. I do not have a financial stake in any business or product mentioned.

Finally, while Bitcoin is global, companies and regulations are not. While I do discuss other countries, this book is mostly intended for an American audience. Therefore, unless I specifically mention another country, you should assume I'm speaking about the US.

If you're ready and excited to learn about Bitcoin, turn the page so we can get started.

Chapter One: SuperMoney

Bitcoin is the first, most popular, and most successful of the cryptocurrencies.

But what exactly does that mean?

Cryptocurrencies are money on steroids. They are the digital equivalent of (and competitor to) more familiar currencies like Dollars, Euros, etc. They use technology and cryptography to provide users with capabilities beyond what can be done with with the monetary and payment systems they're accustomed to. Cryptocurrencies are to money what superheroes are to regular people.

So how exactly are they better?

Cryptocurrencies are bulletproof. By that, I mean they are resistant to interference by third parties. Bitcoin transactions operate like cash over the internet. Once the transaction is confirmed, the BTC is **yours**... 100% resistant to banks, payment processors, lawyers, politicians, or men with guns who may want to meddle with the transaction without your permission. Your funds are as secure as money in your pocket... something that is demonstrably untrue with credit cards and Paypal.

Cryptocurrencies are unstoppable. No one can stop you from doing business with another person using a cryptocurrency such as Bitcoin. The same is true for cash... but you can't use cash over the internet. The introduction to this book mentioned two examples (Wikileaks and BPI) where some entity stood in the way of people conducting transactions with one another. Bitcoin makes such interference impossible. Shutting down Bitcoin would require shutting down the internet as a whole.

Cryptocurrencies are fast. People who've used Bitcoin may be raising their hands to object here. After all, a Bitcoin transaction make minutes to hours to confirm, while a credit card transaction goes through in seconds. But that's not exactly a fair comparison. When you buy something with a credit or debit card, that transaction is approved in seconds... but money doesn't actually change hands (from the credit card company to the merchant) until several days after the purchase. This delay is invisible to the purchaser, making it seem like everything happened in the blink of an eye while the merchant only has the promise of money to be received days later. Cryptocurrencies like Bitcoin don't hide that delay... but the delay is only a few minutes or hours vs several days. For a purchaser this is no big deal. But the merchant standing across the counter from them has suddenly started paying attention.

Cryptocurrencies are intelligent. Cryptocurrencies have scripting capabilities that enable them to do things that cash cannot, such as multi-key transactions that require multiple people to spend from an account, or payment channels that allow frequent transactions among parties without each transaction being recorded to the ledger. Someone just using cryptocurrency to make purchases or send money overseas may not be interested in these more esoteric superpowers, but the ability to create "rules" under which money must be spent is a big deal to businesses, banks, and other financial entities that have been eying blockchain technology (i.e. cryptocurrencies) for some time.

There are more, of course, and not all cryptocurrencies are equally strong in each area. That's the whole point. One of the distinguishing features of Bitcoin spin-off Litecoin is its shorter transaction time. Litecoin is faster. One of the main differences between Ethereum and Bitcoin is that Ethereum has a more robust scripting language... it is "smarter". But Bitcoin is the original, most valuable, and most popular. If cryptocurrencies were superheroes... Bitcoin would be Superman.

How it Works

While conventional currencies are backed up by financial or government institutions, cryptocurrencies are backed by one of the most favorite subjects of students the world over: math. Cryptocurrencies use a dispersed network of computers that allows for what's called a peer-to-peer (P2P) method of transacting. A P2P system is one that doesn't require the services of a middleman or an agent. With Bitcoin and most other cryptocurrencies, this P2P system makes use of a public distributed ledger (blockchain) and mathematical algorithms (encryption and hashing) to maintain security and the integrity of the ledger.

Each account ("Bitcoin address") has an associated secret code ("private key") that the system uses to assert that address's control over the bitcoin the address contains. When bitcoin is spent, the address must provide its private key. Fortunately, most end users don't work with the keys directly and will probably never see one. The wallet software and the Bitcoin network handles all that for them.

Each Bitcoin transaction is simply a record of how currency has moved from a set of source addresses to a set of destination addresses. The Bitcoin protocol performs a number of actions... verifying that the source addresses actually controls the BTC being moved, for instance... and then writes the transaction to the blockchain.

Special Bitcoin users called "miners" are responsible for writing the transactions. This isn't as simple or straightforward as it sounds. Each miner or group (pool) of miners is constantly working on a specific mathematical problem. Not only is this problem difficult, it actually becomes MORE difficult as more people try to solve it. The first to solve the problem correctly gets to write the next block of transactions to the ledger. In return for their effort, they earn some newly created bitcoin, plus they get to keep all the transaction fees in the block they just wrote. In the case of a mining pool, this reward is distributed to the members in the pool, usually based on the amount of work each member contributed. The miner that writes the block gets to pick which transactions get written... and it's in their best interest to pick the transactions that have transaction fees associated with them. Thus, while the transaction fees are technically optional, if you want the miners to care enough about your transaction to write it, you should always include the appropriate fee. All of this applies to Bitcoin, but most other cryptocurrencies operate similarly, with differences in the exact math problem being solved, how the difficulty scales, how miners are rewarded, etc.

Most, but not all, cryptocurrencies have a cap on their maximum number of currency units. For Bitcoin, this is 21 million. Other altcoins have higher, lower, or no cap at all. The mining process above introduces new bitcoin slowly over time until the cap is reached. This process is much more controlled, gradual, and predictable than fiat currencies, which have no cap and no limit to their rate of increase.

Chapter Two: Power and Responsibility

Bitcoin was created by Satoshi Nakamoto (a pseudonym) in 2008. His intention was to give the world a digital currency with no central governing or controlling body, and resistance to interference from 3rd parties like banks, payment processors, and, yes... governments. Within this system, every user is their own bank. Every user has 100% control over their money. But along with this power comes some heightened responsibilities.

Autonomy

With Bitcoin you don't need anyone's consent or permission to spend your money. Not your parent's, not your government's, not your bank's. Unlike traditional bank accounts that your government can "freeze" or hold, your Bitcoin wallets are impervious to such actions by monetary authorities.

The Bitcoin autonomy doesn't end with just the financial transactions. It also extends to your privacy. With credit card companies, you are required to divulge your personal information if you want to use their payment system. But not Bitcoin, which allows you to keep your privacy intact. To be clear... you will probably need to identify yourself to an exchange when you purchase bitcoin, but after that initial purchase the movement of BTC among people is free of personally identifying information. You don't need to give your name and address to a vendor to buy something (unless, of course, they're shipping something to you). Every time you hear about a major retailer getting hacked and their customer's payment data being released, remember that with Bitcoin, there was no need for them to even have that data.

Because Bitcoin is a decentralized monetary system, geographic or legal restrictions won't prevent you from doing business with whoever you want, whenever you want, for whatever you want. This doesn't mean that Bitcoin makes illegal things legal... it means that it's up to YOU to obey the law.

Unique Transactional Features of Bitcoin

Bitcoin has unique features that set it apart from the traditional, centralized monetary systems people are used to. One of them is irreversibility. Once your transaction is written to the blockchain it cannot be canceled, reversed or modified. That's why, when transacting with bitcoin, you must ensure accuracy and security. Bitcoin is like cash in this respect. If you give someone a twenty dollar bill instead of a five and don't realize it until later, you are most likely out of luck. There's no way to "reverse" the cash payment and fix the error. Ditto for Bitcoin.

Another transactional feature is pseudo-anonymity. Bitcoin addresses are random chains of about 30 characters. Your addresses and transactions are innately tied your real-world identity. There is some ambiguity in that last sentence, so let's clarify with some examples:

If you buy something from an online store that needs to be shipped to you, the vendor knows your name and physical address. They also know your Bitcoin address, and can easily connect one with the other. The same is true of exchanges where you buy your bitcoin. They know who you really are and what address they sent bitcoin to. But this connection isn't part of the Bitcoin protocol, it exists outside of it... it comes from the need of the vendor to mail you something, and the legal requirement of the exchange to verify your identity.

You may remember me defining the Bitcoin blockchain as public distributed ledger. Did you catch the word 'public' in that description? It means exactly what you think: your transactions are visible to anyone who cares to look. Total strangers. Your nosy neighbor. The IRS. Anyone. What they'll see is bitcoins moving between addresses. They won't see names, social security numbers, or the fact that you bought condoms at the corner market last night. They won't know which addresses are yours unless you've told them or you've been careless in your use of Bitcoin. Your transactions can be analyzed and traced, but exposing your real identity is quite difficult, and can be made more difficult with some simple steps that I'll talk about in a later chapter.

Another key transactional feature of Bitcoin is security. Your bitcoin can only be accessed by a person who knows the private key of your account, which is you! Technically, your private keys are in your Bitcoin wallet. The wallet should have a password. The phone or computer holding your wallet should be secure. It's up to you to make those things happen. Remember: you are the bank. Powerful cryptography makes it much harder to hack your Bitcoin account compared to traditional bank or credit card accounts.... But if you have a bad password, all that encryption is powerless. The most powerful deadbolt in the world is no good if the door is rotten or the lock isn't fully engaged. However, if you take your duties as the "Bank of Your Own Money" seriously, you gain a truly amazing power: Bulletproof Finances.

Potential Challenges

While Bitcoin offers substantial advantages, it also has its share of challenges. Many of them are not vulnerabilities of Bitcoin itself, but rather of associated businesses, technologies, or people whose weaknesses or actions reflect badly on cryptocurrency as a whole.

Scams and Hacks are a perfect example of this. As soon as bitcoin obtained a monetary value, people began trying to take it from others through theft or fraud. Because Bitcoin is new, some users are unaccustomed to treating it as real money... even though it is. As a result, they fall victim to schemes and scams that they would never fall for if they were dealing with dollars or Euros. Here are some common examples:

Cloud Mining Scams: These are schemes where fictitious companies will propose mining bitcoin on your behalf in exchange for a substantial payment. After paying them, they'll disappear with your money. Note: cloud mining is not ITSELF a scam. There are legitimate cloud mining companies... but if you are new to Bitcoin you should probably avoid them as well. Cloud mining contracts are generally not worth it.

Online Wallets: Here, a company asks you to trust them with your private keys. Instead of using a wallet that YOU control, you use one that THEY control. And then the online wallet gets hacked. Sometimes the "hack" may be a ruse, and the wallet operator has run off with your bitcoin. Millions of dollars have disappeared just like this.

Exchange Scams/Hacks: Exchanges are where you buy/sell bitcoin and other cryptocurrencies. An exchange that is an outright fake is rare... but certainly possible. What you'll most likely see is a legitimate exchange that is careless with their security and gets hacked. Exchanges are like stealth online wallets. When you buy bitcoin, your purchase is stored on the exchange in a wallet that they control. Remember the previous paragraph about Online Wallets? The same applies here. The problem is most people don't realize or consider the exchange to be a wallet... and some exchanges actually encourage you to use their wallet. Don't. Exchanges are for buying... not storing or transacting.

Ponzi Schemes: These are typically ultra-high yield investment schemes that offer you outrageously high and guaranteed yields on your Bitcoin investments. The red flags here are the words "high" and "guaranteed" because the cardinal law in all investments is that the higher your expected return or yield, the higher the risk you must be willing to take. There's no such thing as zero-risk investment that offers yields or returns that are much better than what traditional investments can offer.

The complexity of Bitcoin is another challenge. For the first few years after Bitcoin's release it was not suitable for the general public... regardless of what some claimed. It was difficult to use, and doing so securely required an understanding of concepts like encryption that most people don't have. The situation is much better now. Bitcoin is easier to used than a credit card in most cases . Problem solved? Not quite. If there is a problem in your transaction... if you forget to include a fee, for instance... it is not clear where to get help, and sometimes the advice received is indecipherable to new users. In other words, Bitcoin is only easy on the surface, where most people will normally operate. But that veneer of simplicity is very thin. If someone has to pull back the curtain for any reason, the full complexity may overwhelm them. This isn't acceptable for some people. Bitcoin needs to be simple even when things don't work right... not just when they do.

The volatility of Bitcoin is another hurdle that keeps many from using or continuing to use it. Because many people are risk averse, they either shy away from or stop using bitcoin after experiencing significant "paper" loss due to the swings in the exchange rate. To be clear: all currencies have swings in value. Bitcoin just has and larger, more frequent ones. For some, this volatility is a problem. Others, however, see opportunities to invest.

Lastly, the increasing popularity of Bitcoin has led to increases in the fees required to validate transactions in a reasonable amount of time. This is an issue with scalability. On average, a block of transactions is written to the blockchain every ten minutes. But a block has a size limit. It can only hold a finite number of transactions, and miners will chose to include transactions with higher fees. This can lead to some transactions languishing in a backlog while several blocks go by without them. There are several technological solutions being considered to solve this problem, from simply increasing the block size limit to changing the protocol so that transactions are smaller, and so on. The debate over these solutions has been contentious, but it is clear that something must be done quickly if Bitcoin is to scale beyond its current size.

Chapter Three: Obtaining Bitcoin

There are a number of ways to obtain bitcoin. Buying BTC on an exchange is as straightforward as exchanging dollars for euros, gold, or anything else. However, Bitcoin's digital nature has given it an aura of mystery. People seek answers on how to obtain Bitcoin as if doing so were some epic quest involving digital sacrifices in secret corners of the internet, all of which must be kept from the all-seeing eyes of the law. None of that is true.

So here, in the most straightforward language possible, are several ways you can get your hands on some bitcoin. As you'll see, there are no secrets or arcane mysteries involved.

Using Exchanges

You can buy bitcoin online using your local currency through exchanges. There are dozens of them, but if you are new to Bitcoin, you should probably stick with the more well-known exchanges.

If you are a resident of the United States, Coinbase (www.coinbase.com) and Kraken (www.kraken.com) are two of the more popular Bitcoin exchanges. You typically pay using credit cards or bank transfers. If you are from the United Kingdom, Bittylicious (bittylicious.com) is a good way to buy your bitcoin, with the caveat that they only do business in the United Kingdom. If you are looking for an exchange that works in different countries within the European Union, Bitstamp (www.bitstamp.com) may be a better alternative for you.

If you live in Australia your best bet would be CoinJar (www.coinjar.com). In neighboring New Zealand, you can visit BitPrime (www.bitprime.co.nz) to get your bitcoin. While it's still a relatively young Bitcoin exchange, it works well with most New Zealand bank accounts.

In China, try OKCoin (www.okcoin.cn) and BTCC (www.btcchina.com), the first and second largest exchanges in that country, respectively.

In India, Unocoin (www.unocoin.com) and Zebpay (www.zebpay.com) are worth checking out.

For other parts of the world, use the search function at BuyBitcoinWorldwide (www.buybitcoinworldwide.com) to find an exchange in your country.

And if you are looking for a way to buy Bitcoins outside of organized exchanges, you can try LocalBitcoins.com, which supports cash, wire transfer, credit card, and PayPal for Bitcoin purchases. LocalBitcoins isn't technically an exchange. Rather than sell BTC to you directly in exchange for dollars, this website facilitates peer-to-peer and sometimes face-to-face exchanges among Bitcoin users. You use the LocalBitcoins website to find someone who is willing to exchange currencies with you directly. Since you're dealing with people you don't know, LocalBitcoins.com offers a risk mitigation system in the form of an escrow service. Use it.

You can also buy bitcoin using other cryptocurrencies or altcoins. Once again, you'll be using an exchange to perform this transaction. The difference is that the exchange might not accept USD or other fiat currencies as payment. You'll need to deposit some other cryptocurrency such as Litecoin or Ether. Examples of this type of exchange include Bittrex (www.bittrex.com) and Shapeshift.io (www.shapeshift.io).

You can also buy bitcoin through local ATMs where legal and available. You can use Coinatmradar.com to locate ATMs where you can buy bitcoin at a location near you. Such ATMs are also referred to as BTMs or Bitcoin Teller Machines.

If you prefer, you can also buy bitcoin in an entirely offline, face-to-face transaction through local Bitcoin meetups. Visit www.meetup.com/topics/bitcoin/all/ and bitcoin.xyz/meetup/ to find one near you.

Earning Bitcoin

You're not limited to merely exchanging one currency for another; you can also obtain bitcoin in exchange for your time, energy and talents. If it sounds like I'm talking about a job, you're almost right. While it is certainly possible to find a full-time job that pays you in bitcoin, such jobs aren't plentiful and this isn't a book on job-hunting. Instead, let's explore some more generally useful options.

Jobs4Bitcoin (www.reddit.com/r/Jobs4Bitcoins/) is a subreddit dedicated to connecting people who want things done with people who want bitcoin for doing things. If you have talent or experience in writing, programming, graphic design, translating, or any number of other areas, you can browse the listings to see if anyone is hiring. Or you can make a post of your own announcing your availability for paying gigs. Be prepared to provide samples of your work.

If you are looking for something a little more structured than a Reddit forum, try Xbtfreelancer (www.xbtfreelancer.com) or Bitgigs (bitgigs.com), which both offer similar services.

Do you have a website that gets a decent amount of traffic? There are numerous bitcoin advertising networks that operate similar to Google Adsense, where you "rent out" portions of your site to online advertisers. Note that your site has to be very popular before you can earn more than a few dollars worth of bitcoin per month. If you're interested check out Anonymous Ads (www.a-ads.com).

Avoid so-called "Bitcoin faucets," which pay you trivial amounts of bitcoin in exchange for viewing web pages. I have yet to see one of these that paid a decent return for your time. Not only do they not pay well, but they use increasingly frustrating "anti-cheat" mechanisms that will raise your blood pressure while you earn those tiny fractions of a cent.

Mining Bitcoin

Recall from a previous chapter that Bitcoin transactions are written to the blockchain by miners. The Bitcoin protocol rewards miners with the fees included in the transactions, and with a "block reward" of 12.5 BTC for each block of transactions. The block reward is how new bitcoin gets added to the economy. Since there is a cap of 21 million BTC, the block reward goes down every few years and will eventually vanish altogether when the cap is reached. Also recall that the Bitcoin protocol makes mining more difficult as more people participate.

The idea of creating money out of thin air with your computer was very attractive to Bitcoin early adopters. So much so that the mining difficulty quickly increased beyond the ability of normal computer hardware to keep up. People used to be able to mine profitably with their desktops or laptops. Within a few years only powerful gaming PCs with expensive graphics cards could turn a profit. Shortly after that, companies started producing specialized hardware that outperformed even these powerful gaming PCs. Then the race was on. Specialized mining hardware has gotten more powerful and more expensive every year... for years.

Because of the increasing requirements and costs of mining, miners have come together to create large "pools." These mining pools combine their individual mining power (or "hashrate"). The resulting bitcoin is shared among members of the pool. This idea suffered from the same fate as solo mining. Even as a group, advances in technology made mining unprofitable for people lacking specialized hardware.

I want to be clear here: Bitcoin mining is still profitable. But not without an up-front investment in specialized mining hardware and a source of cheap (or free) electricity to run and cool that hardware. So, while it is still technically possible to mine bitcoin with whatever PC you have on your desk, the current level of competition and the resulting difficulty make this a waste of time and electricity. Don't bother.

If you are still determined to make some of this "magic internet money" the hard (and expensive) way, here's what you'll need to do:

First you'll need to buy some hardware. The actual purchase should be done last, but you need to take a look at what's available and get a feel for how much mining power you can afford to buy. Bitmain has been producing specialized Bitcoin mining hardware for quite some time, but there are other vendors as well. There is a list of Bitmain's products at shop.bitmain.com/main.htm. When you visit, you need to look at more than just the price. You need to note the hashrates, usually given in mega-hashes per second (MH/s) or tera-hashes per second (TH/s), and the power consumption. You'll also need to pay attention to the availability dates, as their website lists items that are not yet in production. Write all of this information down for the unit(s) you can afford, but do not buy anything yet.

Next you'll need to figure out how much your electricity costs. Bitcoin miners run on electricity. The more powerful the hardware, the higher it will drive your electric bill. This isn't a cost you can ignore. Look at your utility bill and figure out your cost in dollars per kilowatt/hour.

Now find the current network hashrate and mining difficulty from a site like BitcoinWisdom (bitcoinwisdom.com/bitcoin/difficulty). These may or may not be necessary for the next step, but they are crucial to your long term profitability. You should know what they mean and how to find the current values.

Since you probably won't be solo mining, find a mining pool. AntPool (www.antpool.com) is a very large, very popular pool, but you should investigate others. Use the mining pool list at Bitcoin Wiki (en.bitcoin.it/wiki/Comparison_of_mining_pools). You'll quickly discover there is more to mining pools than you first imagined. For now, take note of any fees that participants have to pay, and whether the pool distributes transaction fees to participants. Learning about "merged mining", "reward types", etc. is homework that you can save until later... just don't actually start mining until you know what these mean.

Next, visit a mining calculator such as Cryptocompare (www.cryptocompare.com/mining/calculator/) or 99Bitcoins (99bitcoins.com/bitcoin-mining-calculator/). At a minimum, you'll need to enter the hardware price, power consumption, hashrate and electricity cost you gathered earlier. Depending on which site you use you may also need to enter the difficulty and/or network hashrate as well as the mining pool fees.

Examine the results you get. The calculator should tell you how much (if any) profit you can expect under the current network conditions with the hardware you selected. If you like what you see...

Think about the future. Just because the calculator says you can make a profit today doesn't guarantee you'll be in the black next year. Or next week. The mining difficulty changes constantly... almost always by increasing. VnBitcoin (www.vnbitcoin.org/bitcoincalculator.php) not only has yet another mining calculator you can use, but it has information on predicted difficulty rates. Play with the numbers and see how long you'll be profitable with the current rate of increase.

If you've done all of this you've accomplished something that most Bitcoin newcomers never even attempt. Most just assume they can mine profitably and are frustrated when reality (and math) teaches them otherwise. You, however, have run the numbers yourself and proven that you can turn a profit. Now it's up to you to actually make it happen. Start shopping around for deals on the hardware you selected and start learning those mining concepts you ignored earlier.

Setting up a Bitcoin miner after you purchase one is beyond the scope of a beginner's guide. Mining isn't for beginners. It isn't difficult, but it certainly isn't simple. It will require patience and a moderate tolerance for frustration. Between the vendor documentation and the various Bitcoin forums you can find plenty of guidance on getting started. The mining forum on Reddit (www.reddit.com/r/BitcoinMining/) is a good place to go if you run into trouble. Happy Mining.

Mining Alternatives

When confronted with the terrible truth that they can't mine bitcoin with their computers, some Bitcoin newcomers start looking for alternatives. They two they most frequently come across are cloud mining and altcoin mining.

Cloud Mining is just like regular Bitcoin mining, except that instead of buying and running the hardware yourself, you're renting it and paying someone else to run it. Companies like Genesis Mining (www.genesis-mining.com) will sell you a mining contract for certain amount of hashrate. The machines remain in their data centers; you keep the profit. I typically warn people away from cloud mining for two reasons. First is that there have been a number of mining scams that have given the cloud mining industry a black eye. It is far too easy to be taken advantage of. Second is the unwillingness of most people to perform the profitability calculations I detailed earlier in this chapter. That process still applies to cloud mining. But instead of crunching the numbers for themselves, too many people take the marketing hype of cloud mining companies at face value. The result is a disappointing return on investment, or a profit that is driven more by the increase in the bitcoin conversion rate rather than the mining process itself. However, if you do the research and calculations, cloud mining could be a viable alternative to buying hardware yourself. But there are no guarantees.

Bitcoin mining may not be profitable with desktop hardware, but Bitcoin isn't the only cryptocurrency around. There are numerous other currencies that can be mined with standard CPUs and GPUs (graphics cards). Of course, the result of this mining effort wouldn't be bitcoin... it would whatever altcoin you were set up to mine. If it was bitcoin you were after, you'd have to use an exchange or service like Shapeshift to make the conversation. You'll also need to take the exchange's fees into account when you do your profitability calculations.

There is a new altcoin mining pool called Nicehash (new.nicehash.com) that makes the process easy by automatically switching your machine to the most profitable of the altcoins it supports. It also coverts your earnings to bitcoin automatically. With a decent GPU you can easily make a few dollars a day with zero effort beyond the initial setup. With great graphics cards and multiple computers, you can make significantly more. Nicehash even calculates and displays your dollars-per-day in the interface to take some of the effort out of profitability calculations. I am in no way affiliated with Nicehash other than being a user, but based on my experience I recommend it for people who have modern gaming computers that sit idle most of the day.

Chapter Four: Spending Bitcoin

Online Merchants

While the number of establishments that accept bitcoin is still limited compared to traditional currencies, it is growing daily. There are far too many Bitcoin-enabled online merchants to list in this book, but some names among the crowd may surprise you. Major online stores that accept bitcoin include Expedia, Shopify, Microsoft, Dell, Overstock, and the popular gaming platform Steam.

Gift Cards

These merchants, also referred to as 3rd party merchants, sell gift cards that you can buy using bitcoin and use to purchase goods online or offline. Think of them as a bridge that connects bitcoin users with merchants that don't accept bitcoin for payments.

The most popular vendor for gift cards is Gyft (www.gyft.com) The number and names of the vendors they support is too long to list, but it contains such names as Amazon.com, Home Depot, Starbucks, Macy's, Best Buy, Lowes, and Target.

Physical Stores

Just because Bitcoin is a product of the digital age doesn't mean you can't use it to shop offline. More and more "brick and mortar" stores all over the world are now accepting bitcoin payments. From building materials to clothes, from coffee and vape shops to restaurants, physical stores are a new frontier for bitcoin acceptance. You can use resources such as Coinmap (coinmap.org) to find offline or physical stores in your area that accept bitcoin wherever you are in the world.

Amazon via Purse.io

Purse.io (www.purse.io) offers a useful and unique service that allows you use bitcoin for items from Amazon.com without having to buy a gift card first. Purse operates similarly to LocalBitcoins, in that it connects people who want to buy something on Amazon (Shoppers) with people who want to turn their currency into bitcoin (Earners).

Shoppers create a public wishlist on Amazon and populate it with the item or items they want to purchase. They share the wishlist on Purse.io's website, and deposit enough BTC to cover the purchase. An Earner will purchase the items on the wishlist and have them shipped directly to the shopper. Once the items are received the Earner is reimbursed via the bitcoin deposited by the Shopper. It sounds much more complicated than it is. The fact that, as a Shopper, you have the ability to obtain items at a substantial discount makes it worth trying at least once.

OpenBazaar

OpenBazaar (www.openbazaar.org) is an internet-based peer-to-peer marketplace where anyone can sell any item for bitcoin. OpenBazaar has been compared to both Ebay and the Silk Road, but it is neither of these things. There are no auctions, only peer-to-peer sales. There is nothing secret, dark, or hidden about it or its listings. Unlike both Ebay and the Silk Road, OpenBazaar does not operate on one server or set of servers that can be located and shut down. The marketplace is decentralized, free to use, free from external interference, and a good place to both earn and spend bitcoin.

The Bitcoin Payment Process

Regardless of whether you are buying something online or through a face-to-face transaction, using Bitcoin is easier than using a credit card in most cases.

The person or website receiving the payment will show you a QR Code like the one below pictured below:

The code may look like random squares, but your Bitcoin wallet can pull the payment address and, usually, the payment amount out of the code. All you'll need to do is open your wallet, click "send" or "scan" and point your camera at the code. If the payment amount wasn't included in the code, you'll need to type that in. If you're buying something online, you might not even need to use the camera at all The QR code (or the page that is displaying it) will often have a link that should open your Bitcoin wallet directly and populate the required fields.

Before you hit the final "send or "pay" button, make sure you are including an appropriate fee.

Wait... fees? Yes. Remember those miners that are processing your transactions with their expensive specialized hardware? One of the ways they get paid is the "optional" fee that you include in your transaction. I put optional in quotes because, while it is technically possible to send a Bitcoin transaction with zero fee, few (if any) wallets will allow you to do so. Worse still, a zero- or low-fee transaction may take weeks to be written to the blockchain, if it is ever written at all.

Most wallets will suggest a fee amount that you should include, and some will give you options for a higher or lower fee, depending on how fast you want the transaction to process. This fee is based on the complexity of the transaction, not the amount of dollars or BTC you're sending. It also changes according to the load on the network. During Bitcoin's history the recommended fee has ranged from a tiny fraction of a cent to over $2. As of this writing, the wallet that I use recommends a fee of $1, but has options ranging from $.62 for a "low priority" transactions to $1.25 for a "high-priority" transaction. Keep in mind that the fee is paid in bitcoin, and the dollar amount of that fee will vary with the exchange rate. Just use one of your wallet's suggestions and you'll be fine.

What happens now depends on what fee you paid, what you bought, and how the merchant chooses to do business. A Bitcoin transaction is not considered "confirmed" until it is written to the blockchain. This may take ten minutes, an hour, or ten days, depending on the fee... but 10 minutes should be the average for a transaction with an appropriate fee.

Is the cashier at the coffee shop going to make you wait ten minutes before they hand over your beverage? Of course not. The cashier's wallet will display the incoming (but unconfirmed) transaction almost instantly after you make the payment. If they're savvy, they'll check to make sure you include a fee, but most likely they'll just hand over your beverage and move on to the next person in line.

On the other hand... what if you just bought a $200 gift card, a $2000 computer, or a $10,000 used car? Is the merchant going to allow you to walk (or drive) away with the merchandise without waiting for a confirmation? Of course not. You can expect to sit and discuss sports or the weather while the transaction confirms. This is one of those times you might opt to include a higher-than-normal fee with your transaction.

Chapter Five: Keeping Bitcoin

Bitcoin Wallets

As with traditional currencies, safekeeping of your bitcoin is of paramount importance. But unlike traditional currencies the job of securing your wealth is entirely on your shoulders. The fact that bitcoin is entirely digital makes securing them even more difficult. People inherently know how to keep physical objects safe. Securing digital files, however, is outside of most people's area of expertise... until they get hacked. With potentially life-changing amounts of money at stake, learning basic Bitcoin security by trial and error is not acceptable. It is imperative you learn how to store your bitcoin before you start buying or investing large amounts.

Bitcoins are stored in addresses. Multiple addresses are collected in and controlled by wallets. Wallets are usually (but not always) software programs running on a phone or computer. With proper safety practices and mechanisms, these wallets can be safer than your physical wallet, bank account, and credit cards. Without these basic security measures, however, bitcoin wallets are like keeping a bag of money half-hidden behind a flowerpot on your front porch.

There are four kinds of Bitcoin wallets that you can choose from: web wallets, software wallets, cold storage wallets, and hardware wallets.

Software or "hot" wallets are the ones you will interact with most often. This is the Bitcoin wallet on your phone or computer that you use for buying, selling, and transferring BTC. There are several companies producing wallets for the various platforms. I recommend Mycelium on Android and Breadwallet on iOS. For PC, I recommend Electrum. My two rules for choosing a wallet are: 1) Do not pay for wallet software. It should be free. 2) Do not store large amounts of money in a hot wallet. Software wallets are the equivalent of petty cash or the money you carry around in your pocket. They are not a savings account, so don't put thousands of dollars into one unless you are about to make a large purchase in the very near future.

A web wallet is a software wallet hosted on an online server and usually accessed through a web browser. There are some very popular and trustworthy companies that will store your bitcoin for you in their online servers. I'm not naming them because you should avoid all of them. That's right... all of them. The <u>short history of Bitcoin</u> is filled with online wallets that got careless or turned out to be scams, resulting in the unreimbursed loss of their clients' funds. Learn from other people's mistakes: **Do Not Store Bitcoin In An Online Wallet**. This includes the wallets run by the exchanges where you buy bitcoin. You can trust them to buy or sell your bitcoin, but you should not trust them to store it for you.

Cold Storage wallets, also referred to as offline wallets, are wallets that are totally removed from a hosting device or the Internet. This can be an old computer or phone that you've loaded some Bitcoin software onto and disconnected from the internet. The average user will typically only put this machine online long enough to transfer funds from the cold wallet into their hot wallet... similar to taking money out of a savings account into a checking account. This is where the bulk of your bitcoin should be kept. Note that the platform... the phone or PC that you are using... must be secure and must only be used for Bitcoin. Wiping the operating system and starting with a fresh, virus-free re-install is recommended. Using the device to browse the web, read books, watch porn, update your resume, or anything else will get your bitcoin stolen out from under you.

Hardware wallets are a special type of cold storage. These are specific hardware devices... physical objects... that you can use to store bitcoin and access it securely even from a computer that isn't itself secure. If you are dealing with life-changing amounts of money, then you should invest in one of these. Otherwise, ordinary cold storage wallets on an old phone or PC may suffice.

Paper wallets are yet another special type of cold storage. As the name suggests, a paper wallet stores your bitcoin address and private key on an ordinary piece of paper. You use a computer and a printer to create the paper wallet and a normal hot wallet to send bitcoin to/from the address encoded on the page. While the bitcoin is at rest it is completely isolated from the internet and invulnerable to attack... unless you loose the paper wallet or didn't follow instructions when you created it. Paper wallets are very useful, and were the only hardware wallets available until companies like Ledger and Trezor came along. But they are not user friendly. They are too easy to use incorrectly, and using them the right way can be awkward. Nevertheless, they are worth exploring if you will be storing large amounts of BTC and don't want to purchase special hardware to do so. They can at the very least be a temporary storage measure while your hardware wallet is being shipped. If you want to play around with paper wallets visit BitAddress (www.bitaddress.org). Warning: Going to a website and printing off a paper wallet is insecure. It's fine for learning and experimenting, but not for actual use. Creating a *secure* paper wallet involves multiple steps and a moderate amount of paranoia. Also, never buy paper wallets from anyone. Always create your own.

Preparing for Bitcoin

Cold storage or hardware wallets either cost money or require you to have an extra machine sitting around that you can dedicate to Bitcoin. Paper wallets are free, but they are confusing and take time to create correctly. These may not be suitable options for everyone, so some may choose to store their bitcoin on their ordinary phone or computer. While this this isn't recommended, it is understandable and almost certainly the route that most new users will take. Given the higher risks associated with software wallets, you will need to exercise extra caution when using them for storing larger amounts.

Entire libraries have been written on how to secure computers. The unfortunate truth is that the average user will never read even one of those books and, if they did, probably wouldn't follow the recommendations it contains. For that reason, I'm going to scale down all of that very good advice to the absolute bare minimum you need to do. If you perform any financial transactions on your phone or PC... either with bitcoin or your regular banking/investing website... you should do the following:

Put a passcode or password on your machine. It doesn't need to be long, but it does need to be complex. Uppercase, lowercase, special characters... the more complex the better. Hopefully, you are already doing this.

Use some kind of anti-virus or anti-malware. If you have Windows, use the Windows Defender that comes with the operating system. There are several for Android; consider Malwarebytes or Lookout. The latter comes already installed on a lot of newer Android devices. Whatever you use, it should not only scan the device periodically for malware on the hard drive, it should also actively monitor activity on the device in an attempt to catch malware in the act.

I find Apple's operating systems for its devices like the MacBook, iPad, and the iPhone to be quite virus and malware-resistant. However, Apple's electronic products are significantly more expensive than Windows-based computer devices, Android phones, and Android tablets.

The last bit of advice is for Windows users only. It is also crucial for that platform. If you are like most people you only have one account on your machine, and that account is an administrator. This means that the account you use while surfing the internet is also able to manage the settings, install software, and make changes to the machine's configuration... exactly the things that a virus or trojan wants to do once it hits your machine. You need to fix that. The account that you use every day should not be an administrator. You need to create a second account that you only log into when you are installing or configuring something. This new account should be the administrator while your everyday computer use should just be done under a "standard" account.

These simple steps, particularly the last one, will go a long way toward making your computer safe enough for financial use.

Choosing and Setting Up a Wallet

Now it's time to choose your Bitcoin software wallet. If you want to do your own research instead of just picking one of the ones I mentioned earlier, go to bitcoin.org/en/choose-your-wallet and click around. All Bitcoin software wallets are not created equal. Even if all the features and security were the same among them, there are still vast differences in initial setup and ease of use. Bitcoin Core, for example, requires you to download the entire Bitcoin blockchain before you can use it. That might sound okay until you realize that the blockchain is over 120GB and will take over a week to download. New users don't need that level of frustration, so I recommend you avoid Bitcoin Core.

After successfully setting up the software wallet in your chosen electronic device, you'll need to work on the software settings before using it. The two most important settings that you should pay attention to are your wallet's password and backup system.

If the software lets you create a PIN or password to access your wallet, you should set one. This should be different from the one you use to unlock your PC, phone or tablet. Your software may also present you with a list of random words that allow you to restore your wallet when needed. Write the words down... physically, on paper... and store them somewhere safe. These random words are literally the keys to your Bitcoin kingdom. Do not store them on (or near) your computer; they belong in a safe, safe deposit box, or other secure storage place that is both fire and waterproof.

Address Management

Once you've set up your first Bitcoin wallet, look for your Bitcoin addresses. All software is different, but since address management is the entire point of the wallet, the software should display them prominently. You have more than one address. If you only see one, rest assured that your wallet can create additional addresses with the click of a button.

When receiving bitcoin, such as when you are transferring newly purchased BTC out of an exchange, you will need to provide one of your address. Please don't try to memorize or type an address by hand, use copy/paste.

You should generate a new address every time you need to receiver bitcoin. **Do Not Re-Use Addresses**. Once you use an address to receive BTC once... forget about it. Don't worry, it's the wallet software's job to keep track of how much BTC is in each address, not yours. Using different addresses makes it more difficult for people to track your Bitcoin activity on the blockchain.

Hardware Wallets

As mentioned earlier, hardware wallets are the most secure way to store your bitcoin. While there aren't as many hardware wallets as software wallets, there are still too many to list and describe in detail. Instead, I'll focus on the two most popular ones.

Trezor (trezor.io) is a dongle that plugs into the USB port of your computer. You access it via your web browser using special software or a browser extension that you obtain from Trezor. The interface is much like a regular software wallet, but behind the scenes it is using a lot of encryption to isolate your wallet (and the bitcoin it contains) from the computer you plug it into. The Trezor retails at $100 on the Trezor website, but supplies are limited and the prices at 3rd party vendors are $175 to $200 USD. When you shop for one, be prepared to find many vendors with limited stock and higher prices.

Ledger (www.ledgerwallet.com) sells the Ledger Nano S as a hardware wallet that operates similarly to the Trezor. It can integrate with existing wallet software such as Mycelium, and be used with a small list altcoins besides Bitcoin, such as Litecoin and Ethereum. It is also slightly cheaper, retailing at $70 on Ledger's website.

For use with Bitcoin, the differences between these two are largely cosmetic. Choose whichever you can afford or whichever you can actually find in stock. If you are doing research online, be aware that Ledger produced a previous version of their hardware wallet that lacked many features. Reviewers generally considered inferior to the Trezor, but those reviews don't apply to the current Ledger Nano S.

When you first get your hardware wallet, do your best to ascertain that it is brand new, i.e., it hasn't been used or tampered in any way prior to your receiving it. There have been instances when customs agents and authorities have opened shipments and in the process, removed security seals of the items contained in such shipments. Remember, your bitcoins' security will depend on the integrity of your hardware wallet and as such, it must arrive on your doorstep in a pristine and unmodified state.

Once you're satisfied that your hardware wallet is genuine and hadn't been tampered with, you'll go through the initial setup that is similar to setting up a software wallet. There are passwords to set and lists of random words to write down. Do so and enjoy using Bitcoin is the most secure way possible.

Chapter Six: Investing in Bitcoin

Disclaimer: *I am not a financial or investment adviser. This chapter is general advice only. It has been prepared without taking into account your objectives, financial situation or needs. Before acting on this advice you should consider its appropriateness in regard to your own objectives, financial situation and needs. Regardless of what I or anyone else says, you should never invest in something you do not understand, or invest funds you cannot afford to lose.*

While Bitcoin was created as an alternative and decentralized mode of payment, it can also be used as an investment. Bitcoin had zero value when it was initially released in January of 2009. Shortly thereafter it had a value of .08 cents per bitcoin, mostly based on the amount of electricity required to mine BTC at the time. In mid-2017 the value of 1 Bitcoin peaked at $3,000.

Upon hearing the previous figures, most people have one of two reactions. Some feel that they have obviously "missed the boat" on Bitcoin and that there's no point in investing now. Others see the exponential rise as an obvious sign that Bitcoin is a scam. Neither of these is true,, but it can be difficult to change minds without delving into Bitcoin's history and the true meaning of its technology.

But first, let's attack some of the more popular objections to Bitcoin investing.

One of the reasons why many people fear investing in, or even using, Bitcoin is the infamous bankruptcy of one of the biggest Bitcoin exchanges in the world, Mt. Gox in 2014, which preceded a precipitous drop in price. Many proclaimed Bitcoin to be "dead" at this point. Yet, Bitcoin still exists and is trading a significantly higher price than it was in 2014. In fact, Bitcoin has "died" so often that it has become a meme or joke in the Bitcoin community. The collapse of Mt Gox is a historical footnote among a sea of other hacks and collapses... none of which have "killed" cryptocurrency. These were not failures of Bitcoin or of cryptocurrency any more than the Cyprus financial crisis of 2012 was a failure of fiat currency.

Another black mark is Bitcoin's association with scams, frauds, and black market activities such as the Bitcoin Savings and Trust Ponzi scheme and the Silk Road dark market. Yet the same people who decry Bitcoin's reputation continue to use a currency with a much longer history of even stronger ties to illegal activity: Cash... the currency of drug dealers, pedophiles, and black markets since before the internet existed. Despite rumors to the contrary, Bitcoin is NOT anonymous and people who use Bitcoin for illegal activities do get caught and convicted. The investigation of their activities just takes a different set of skills. Criminals who are serious about keeping their transactions under the radar will do as they always have... use cash.

Another reason for the skepticism is the high volatility in the market value or prices of Bitcoin, which is about 2,600% more volatile than investing in the S&P 500, one of the biggest stock exchanges in the United States and in the world. Yes, Bitcoin is volatile. But that volatility isn't just random noise... it has a very sharp upward trend with discernible patterns. This is what true investors call an opportunity.

And finally, Bitcoin's lack of regulatory body or agency scares people. It's hard for an outsider to see who controls Bitcoin. Is it the government? The Federal Reserve? The Bitcoin Foundation? The mysterious Satoshi Nakamoto? No. Bitcoin (the technology) is controlled by the actions of the developers, miners and users... the Bitcoin community. The bitcoin price is controlled by the free market forces of supply and demand. Let's not forget that the maximum supply of Bitcoin is known and capped at $21 million. The maximum number of US Dollars is infinite. This makes Bitcoin fundamentally different from all traditional currencies. It is more akin to gold and silver, with advantages of being more resistant to government and corporate interference and being able to be used over the internet.

Given the above, should you use Bitcoin for investing purposes? Unfortunately, the answer is neither clear nor simple. The short version of the answer is: "It Depends". The long answer is that, you'll need to consider several things about your own goals, financial situation, and personality before making a decision.

Financial Timeline

While it's obvious that the goal of investing is to make more money, that is a very general goal and is insufficient for actually making investment decisions.

You need to be specific in your expected return, and even more so in your time frame. Are you investing money so you can have a retirement fund in twenty years? Is it for your kids' college education in ten years? Or is it for the new car you're going to buy in a few months?

Bitcoin is NOT a suitable short term investment. If you need to jump in and out of your investment in time frames shorter than a year, you'd be better off looking elsewhere. Bitcoin's strength is its long-term trend. In the short term, the volatility could bite you. Hard. I consider short-term Bitcoin investing to be the same as gambling. Yes, people make money day trading or short-term investing in bitcoin. People also win at blackjack.

If, however, your investment timeline is measured in years, then Bitcoin might be for you.

Risk Appetite

Bitcoin is a high-risk investment. Don't let anyone tell you otherwise.

How much money are you comfortable losing? No one intends to lose money, but all investments have risks. The only question is how much risk can you take. If you want to earn substantially higher returns, you must be willing to accept more risk. Experienced investors know this, but Bitcoin has a tendency to attract inexperienced or amateur investors who expect high returns without the potential for loss. Don't be an amateur. If you ARE an amateur... Bitcoin probably isn't for you. Bitcoin should not be the first or only investment in your portfolio.

If you prefer investments whose returns are guaranteed, consider Treasury Bonds issued by the Federal Government. However, you must be willing to settle for rates of return so low that you may actually lose money because of inflation. But if you are willing to take on higher investment risks to earn potentially higher returns, then you can invest your money in riskier assets like stocks and bitcoin.

Emotional Stability

Suppose you bought some bitcoin today at $2500, and tomorrow the price drops to $1400. It may not be likely, but stranger things have certainly happened. Whether you sell or hold depends on your investment strategy, but that's not the question I'm asking. What about you? Can you handle the emotional reaction to such a stunning potential loss? How would you handle it? Would you panic? Would you take it in stride and move on? Would you obsess over the price, checking it constantly in search of validation? Would you ask, then beg, then plead with strangers on the internet to magically predict when the price will go back up? Would you sink into depression? Would you consider harming yourself?

This may be an unexpectedly dark section to find in a chapter on investment, but some people are emotionally unprepared for the stunning losses that have occurred in Bitcoin's past. As I said earlier, Bitcoin tends to attract people who are new to investing These people tend to invest too much and are not capable of maintaining perspective if things don't go their way. Don't be one of them. There are more important things in the world than money... Bitcoin or otherwise. If your happiness, your survival, your financial or emotional stability depend on the price of an investment behaving in a certain manner... please stay away from Bitcoin.

Timing

Lastly, one universal aspect of trading in financial assets like stocks, currencies, and of course bitcoin, is knowing when to get in and when to get out. There are two approaches to investing that you can take: a buy-and-hold approach and a trading approach.

A buy-and-hold approach is one where you buy bitcoin and wait for its value to go up over the medium to long term. It's also called a buy-it-and-forget-it approach because you don't need to concern yourself with daily or even weekly fluctuations. This approach requires a long-term mindset and, in the specific case of bitcoin, nerves of steel as you wait out short term drops in value. With Bitcoin, those short-term drops can be quite dramatic.

The trading approach is a very short-term one, where you get in and out of bitcoin in a few days, hours, or even minutes. Some people make a killing out of this approach but this requires a lot of time and effort to monitor and execute. It is not for amateurs, and I don't even recommend it for professional traders unless they've educated themselves on the history and technology of Bitcoin.

But even if you take the buy-and-hold approach, it doesn't mean you're off the hook in terms of timing your entry into the market. Should you invest everything at once, or invest over time? Should you buy right now at whatever the price happens to be, or wait until one of those short-term drops?

The answer depends on how much risk you can swallow, financially and emotionally.

If you have a lump sum and won't be shaken by an unexpected drop, invest all at once. You are missing out on potential gains if you wait. If you don't have a lump sum, or the idea of a $400 price drop after you hit "buy" scares you, then invest a specific dollar amount every week or month until you reach your investment goal... but start right now.

Holding your dollars waiting for a short-term drop is generally a bad idea. You don't know how long you'll be waiting, or whether the price dip you are expecting will happen at all. Either buy now, or buy over time beginning right now. I also don't recommend borrowing money to invest in BTC. Don't mortgage your house. Don't take out a bank loan or borrow against your retirement plan. You either have the money to invest or you don't. If you don't, then buying over time is your best option.

In short: *The best time to buy bitcoin was 2009. The second best time to buy bitcoin is right now.*

And finally, once you've acquired Bitcoins for the purpose of investing, be sure to follow the safety protocols for storing your bitcoin that I've outlined earlier in the book. For long-term storage of large amounts, use a cold wallet, hardware wallet, or paper wallet. Storing your investment on a phone wallet is *extremely* unwise.

Author's Notes: What's Next?

Thank you for buying this book. My goal in writing it was to provide enough basic guidance to get you started with Bitcoin... or at least enough to get you interested. I urge you now to take action on what you've learned. Regardless of whether you are a potential investor, merchant, miner, developer or educator, your next steps are the same. Ready? Here they are:

Buy some bitcoin. Spend some of it. Save the rest.

That's it. Doing this with just a small amount of bitcoin, $10 to $100 dollars worth, will start cementing and internalizing what you've learned in this book. You'll work with an exchange. You'll find and install a wallet. You'll locate a merchant that accepts bitcoin in exchange for something you want. You'll experience the importance of fees. And you'll have a tiny bit of bitcoin stashed away in case of another 10- or 100-fold increase in value. All of this was described in this book, but no amount of explanation is as good as firsthand experience. So go ahead... use Bitcoin the way it was meant to be used. From there you can branch out into your specific areas of interest, be it mining or investing, starting a bitcoin-based business or charity, or using Bitcoin to send money overseas.

Even if you decide Bitcoin isn't for you, you'll have made that decision based on personal experience rather than a preconceived notion. Don't worry, cryptocurrencies like Bitcoin aren't going anywhere. They'll still be here when you change your mind. And you *will* change your mind.

Until then,

Thanks for Reading

Eric Morse

Ethereum:
A Primer

Your Guide to Understanding, Using, And Profiting from the Digital Currency That's Smarter Than Bitcoin

By

Eric Morse

To those who dare to build upon the shoulders of giants.

Introduction

What is Ethereum?

What's so special about it?

You might have been following Bitcoin for some time, but never quite grasped the concept of Ethereum. After all, some alternative cryptocurrencies (or "altcoins") are just clones of Bitcoin, while others appear to be vastly different and much harder to understand. Ethereum seems to fall into the later category... but how, exactly, is it different?

Perhaps you have only heard of Ethereum recently due to its phenomenal price jump in the past few months. You want to know what this investment is, what gives it value, and if there is still any upward potential remaining. In other words: Why are people buying it?

Regardless of what category you're in; your questions will be explained in this book.

Let's start with Bitcoin. You might see it with a lowercase "b" when talking about the currency, or an uppercase B when referring to the payment network on which the currency is used. At its core, Bitcoin is a distributed public ledger called the blockchain, with the associated programming necessary to add and verify transactions. Bitcoin has a scripting language that is used to create transactions that move the bitcoin (note the lowercase) from one person to another. However, there is a shortcoming. While Bitcoin might seem quite complex and powerful, in terms of computer science it has a stunning weakness: it is not Turing-complete. This is just a fancy way of saying that the programming language behind Bitcoin too limited, and thus incapable of performing very complex transactions. In other words: Bitcoin, while powerful, isn't too bright.

Ethereum is the smarter Bitcoin.

The most significant difference between Ethereum and Bitcoin is the purpose and the capability of the two networks. Bitcoin offers a specific blockchain application, that of a peer-to-peer digital cash system. The system allows for online payments of a digital currency that is also called "bitcoin" (abbreviated "BTC"). This network is used for tracking the ownership of the bitcoin currency, but Ethereum is focused on the program code needed to run a decentralized application. To over-simplify it: Bitcoin is all about the blockchain and transactions, while Ethereum focuses on the code. Bitcoin could replace Paypal and Visa. Ethereum could replace insurance companies, venture capital firms, and much of the legal infrastructure that relates to contract law.

Ethereum is a platform upon which other things can be built. Specifically, it is a blockchain-based open-source platform that gives developers the opportunity to build and deploy decentralized applications. Like Bitcoin, it has a distributed public ledger... a blockchain. It also has a currency called "ether" (abbreviated "ETH"). But rather than being spent in the same way as we can make purchases with bitcoin, ether is the fuel that is needed to run programs on Ethereum. Ether can be traded. It has a dollar value. But is generally used by the application developers to pay for the services and the transaction fees on the Ethereum network. You are unlikely to buy a cup of coffee, a car, or a house with ether. But, in the future, your mortgage (or your mortgage company) may be written in code that consumes ether to run on the Ethereum blockchain.

But what does this actually mean in practice? What does Ethereum do with these extra capabilities? More importantly, what can we mere humans do with these capabilities?

Read on...

Chapter 1: What Is Ethereum

Before we launch into our exploration of Ethereum, we need to define some terms and concepts:

Smart Contracts

There's no real difference between a "smart contract" and a normal contract in the traditional sense. They are both agreements that certain parties will perform specific actions under specific circumstances. A Smart Contract is a piece of computer code that contains instructions for a transaction that takes place *only* when certain conditions are met.

All blockchains can process code but most of them are limited in what they can do. That is where Ethereum differs; instead of developers being limited as they are with Bitcoin complexity, they can be built systems of transactions so complex that they can mimic the operation of an entire corporation. More on that later.

You can liken contracts in Ethereum to programmable bank accounts that you can interact with via transactions on the Ethereum network.. While contracts in the real world require the oversight of attorneys or legal professionals to be enacted, in the crypto-world this is not so. This allows for lower expenses, and fewer requirements to be entered into the transaction.

Whenever you sign your name on a sales receipt or click the "I understand" radio button when buying a product or service, you are entering into a contract similar to what you might encounter in Ethereum. However, Ethereum contracts can be enacted by anyone and all users can interact with them in an open manner (similar to simple transaction 'contracts' that move ETH from one person to another). These smart contracts are basically a computer program that has been written in one of the Ethereum high-level programming languages. The primary languages are Solidity or Serpent, but others can be used. Once written, the program is entered into a special transaction along with a minimal transaction fee, payable in Ethereum's currency: ether.

What benefits do smart contracts give us?

Efficiency: In our current legal system, most contracts are written is incredibly complex, yet still open to interpretation. If you and the other party differ on interpretations of a certain contract, the process becomes difficult to thresh out and will likely require court cases or legal mediation. With smart contracts, the contract is written in a logical, almost mathematical way where interpretation is no longer necessary. The question of which party has the correct legal basis is no longer open to discussion or interpretation. Once the contract is deployed into the blockchain, the contract is secured and the execution of the contract will take place in a logical, rational, and mathematical process.

Autonomy: Because they are programmed to run on the blockchain, these contracts execute exactly how and when they are written without the reliance (or interference) of third-parties. They are not interpreted or enforced by judges, courts, or governments... they are enforced by the Ethereum network.

The Virtual Machine

The core innovation of Ethereum is the EVM or Ethereum Virtual Machine. It is a Turing-complete software running on the Ethereum network, enabling anyone to run whatever program they want, as long as they have the ether to fuel its operation. The EVM simplifies the process of creating blockchain-based applications and makes it more efficient. Rather than needing to build a new blockchain for each application, the EVM enables thousands of different apps to be built on one platform.

Prior to Ethereum, designers and innovators seeking to create new blockchain applications had two choices:

The first was to construct an application on top of Bitcoin. Unfortunately, Bitcoin's scripting language is very limited compared to other languages like C++. While Bitcoin has been modified many times since its inception, attempts to increase the capabilities of its script were either not successful, or not sufficient. The end result is that Bitcoin simply cannot do what some developers want it to do, and attempts to make it more capable are resisted for a variety of reasons.

The other choice was to create your own cryptocurrency. Bitcoin is open-source, making it quite easy for anyone with sufficient skill to take the code and modify it to make something new. This has been done many times, with some of the early altcoins being little more than clones of Bitcoin with slightly different operating parameters. Making a Bitcoin clone for each new application or feature seems like the preferred solution until you realize that each clone needs miners, users, wallets, exchange support, community support... all the things that Bitcoin already has. Reproducing even a fraction of Bitcoin's ecosystem takes time, energy, and money... and success is in no way guaranteed.

Ethereum took an approach that incorporates both potential solutions. Yes, Ethereum is an altcoin. It was a new cryptocurrency that required miners, wallets, etc... everything that Bitcoin already had. BUT, the Ethereum developers wanted to do this work just once. They wanted to create one altcoin with a robust scripting language upon which developers could build whatever they wanted. These new applications wouldn't require their own blockchains, miners, etc., because they'd be using Ethereum's. Now, anyone could develop any application and use the Ethereum system to execute it. All without building their own cryptocurrency from the ground up.

The potential uses of such a framework are boundless. One of the more obvious uses is making digital currencies in only a few dozen lines of code and releasing them on the Ethereum blockchain. This requires a lot less work and a lot less infrastructure than the "hard way" of cloning Bitcoin... and this is exactly what has happened. Later on we'll look at some very ambitious cryptocurrency projects that went this route. For now, just realize that, like "smart contracts," the platform for building other applications is one of the key concepts of Ethereum.

What Can We Use Ethereum For?

Ethereum is primarily intended for developers to use to build and deploy their decentralized applications. Otherwise known as Dapps (for "Decentralized APPlication"), these applications usually serve a very specific purpose... to fill some niche currently dominated by a non-blockchain solution. Bitcoin is a Dapp that provides a P2P digital cash that competes with government-backed "fiat" currency. Because these applications are comprised of code that runs on the blockchain, no one person or entity controls them. Just like Bitcoin is not controlled by the Federal Reserve, the European Union, or the Bank of England... an Ethereum-based Dapp that fills some "contract law" niche would exist outside of the jurisdictions of any nation. Parties not involved in the contract (Lawyers, judges, politicians...) could not alter or impede its operation. Sure, they can seize property or inflict punishment after the fact, but they can't stop the contract from executing as originally written. Now imagine this concept extended to other services like banking, insurance, arbitration, regulatory compliance, or voting. Almost any service that is currently centralized can easily be decentralized with Ethereum... even many services currently provided by governments.

We can also use Ethereum to build DAOs – Decentralized Autonomous Organizations. This is another key concept. These are decentralized organizations that are fully autonomous, having no one leader. They are run purely by networks of smart contracts that have been written on Ethereum. This code replaces the structure and the rules of a traditional organization and eliminates the need for centralized control. Each DAO is owned by those who purchase Ethereum-based tokens that provide the token owner with voting rights. Think of a corporation engaged in a specific line of business... car insurance, for instance. Remove all of the humans from that corporation, and turn all the business rules and contracts (or insurance polices in this example) into smart contracts. That is a DAO. Yes, there are still people involved in some processes, but for the most part those people are just providing inputs (underwriting data) and receiving outputs (insurance claims checks). They are not making decisions. They are not changing (or breaking) procedures. They are not responsible for making sure the company runs according to its rules. Ethereum is doing that.

And because these decentralized applications will run on the blockchain, they will all benefit from the properties of the common to most cryptocurrencies:

Immutable - changes cannot be made to any data by a third party. Transactions cannot be reversed unless that capability is built into the contracts.

Secure – all applications and transactions are secured with cryptography, giving them strong protection against fraud and hacking.

No Downtime – the blockchain is distributed across the network of machines running Ethereum. Apps built upon it can't go down and cannot be switched off... again, unless that capability is built into its design.

The Real Benefits of Ethereum

Think once again back to our insurance company implemented without employees via a DAO. Its operating costs would become significantly smaller than competitors that still relied on flesh-and-blood lawyers and underwriters. But it would still have costs. The cost in Ethereum is called "gas" and it is a universally accepted expense for performing any computational work using the Ethereum. Gas has a consistent cost, regardless of the volatility of Ether's value, helping to stabilize the currency and provide more efficient paths for coding the contracts. In reality, the real value of Ethereum's platform is to create a system in which methodologies can be founded on for running business transactions with more efficient costs and timeframes.

For instance, some vendors (particularly gas stations) have a minimum purchase amount for using a credit card. It might be $5, or $2... or maybe 99cents. Why is that? That amount is directly related to the cost of transferring your account's balance to another account's balance. There is always a net loss of money from any transaction between two parties, because some fees automatically to go to the network in charge of moving that money (such as Visa, Master Card, American Express, etc). This cost becomes prohibitive for micro transactions. It also accumulates quickly as the number of transactions increase. In other words, it costs them more than 99cents to receive 99cents in payment via credit cards. This is as true for cryptocurrencies as it is for traditional money... but the fees are lower, and the currency is infinitely divisible.

Let's clarify look at an example. Currently, it is impossible to pay for streaming video services per the number of seconds you watch. If you were to open a transaction or contract to watch only a second of video and then close the transaction afterward, the resulting payment would be less than one cent. Possibly much less. The US Dollar is not divisible to that amount... but Bitcoin, Ethereum, and most other cryptocurrencies are. There's also the matter of fees, which would completely overwhelm the amount of the transaction itself.

This issue is circumvented with cryptocurrencies. Incredibly small transaction amounts are not a problem, and transaction costs are (or can be) minimized using smart contracts, projects like the Lightning Network, other methods not available in traditional currencies. Compared to Bitcoin, Ethereum is more suited for the infrastructure of businesses and intelligently designed contracts for most business needs and financial transactions. It can be thought of as an alternative to the office building with cubicles. Its infrastructure was especially designed with this in mind, as a "black box" in which to operate transactions and store data.

Chapter 2: A Short History Lesson

Let's take a look at Ethereum's history.

In 2013 a Bitcoin programmer named Vitalik Buterin wanted to expand on the intelligence and decentralized nature of Bitcoin. Part of the problem Mr. Buterin saw with Bitcoin was that it was becoming too centralized. Bitcoin's popularity was growing fast, mainly due to its perceived value as a store of wealth and its potential to supplant systems like Paypal, Visa... and even fiat currencies. What really drew people's attention was the concept of mining.

Mining is the process by which new transactions are written to the blockchain. The process is difficult and becomes even more difficult (requiring more powerful computers) as more people participate. Why would anyone want to? Money. The system rewards successful miners with Bitcoin. Mining was always meant to be a distributed process, but the idea of using a computer to turn electricity into digital gold proved too tempting. As more people poured into the mining ecosystem, it became so difficult that only large groups people with expensive specialized hardware could compete. Solo hobbyists couldn't keep up. Bitcoin mining was now an industry... an industry with few participants, each of which having a large influence over the Bitcoin network. In other words, Bitcoin was becoming centralized. Buterin felt this centralization was contrary to Bitcoin's core goals, and he also felt that Bitcoin could be more useful it was smarter and wasn't focused almost exclusively on one application: replacing cash.

So in March of 2014, Ethereum debuted as a project that could extend blockchain use beyond the traditional peer-to-peer transactions. While legal issues and questions arose to both its legality and technical feasibility, it soon became apparent that it was a legitimate project after Buterin won the "World Technology Award" for the creation of Ethereum.

A major crowdfunding effort for the project began in July of 2014. Investors converted their bitcoin to Ethereum tokens, raising 3,700 BTC (2.3 million USD) on the first day. When crowdfunding ended in September, Buterin and his Ethereum Project had raised $20million from Bitcoin purchases alone.

By the end of May 2016, Ethereum market value quickly rose to more than 1 billion USD. It was quickly becoming a serious contender against Bitcoin itself.

One of the first major projects built on the Ethereum network was a venture capital fund referred to as "The DAO." We already introduced the concept of a Decentralized Autonomous Organization, so the name of this project should be both familiar and confusing. There can be any number of DAOs, but in this case we are referring to a *specific* organization, which simply called itself The DAO.

The DAO comprised the largest bundle of smart contracts on Ethereum and was the earliest, most publicized project on the platform. Its purpose was to collect money from investors and distribute it to projects that the investors voted on... similar to a venture capital firm. The DAO's operation was contained entirely on the Ethereum blockchain. It did not have a street address. It didn't have a Board of Directors. It was not incorporated under the laws of any nation or government. The DAO was just a set of rules and procedures codified in contracts stored in the blockchain. The DAO was so large, in fact, that it was able to raise roughly 170 million dollars in Ethereum tokens from investors.

Unfortunately, there were security flaws in The DAO's smart contracts, which enabled hackers to steal 3.6 million ETH-roughly $50 million at the time-and transfer it to different accounts. So much had been invested and stolen that the Ethereum community was vehement about action being taken. There were contentious debates about two options: a soft fork, wherein the pilfered currency would be "burned" or made unusable by either the thieves or the original owners, and a hard fork or a total rollback of the blockchain to a point before the exploit occurred, resulting in a kind of alternate timeline. A soft fork would maintain the blockchain in its original form, complete with The DAO's creation and the multi-million-dollar exploit. A hard fork would go back in time and create a new reality where the DAO exploit never happened.

Vitalik and the other Ethereum developers favored a hard fork which was the action eventually taken. However, many Ethereum users disagreed with this decision, as they believed in the concept of the blockchain being immutable and permanent. As a result, they created a version of Ethereum on the unaltered blockchain, which they called Ethereum Classic (ETC). Although the two versions of Ethereum share a common beginning, there are incompatible with each other.

Ethereum Classic is still a major cryptocurrency and, while it lags behind Bitcoin, Ethereum and Litecoin in value, it is still in the top 10 in terms of market capitalization (as of the time of writing).

Despite this early drama, Ethereum remains one of the most technologically innovative forms of cryptocurrency and shows no signs of slowing down. Some day, a cryptocurrency may overtake Bitcoin and Ethereum just might be the one to do it.

Chapter 3: A Currency for the Future

Now you have an understanding of what Ethereum is and where it came from... what can it do? What applications are being developed that make it worth investing time and money into? Currently, the majority of the use cases involve transmitting financial data. Many of the Ethereum apps that are in development, however, are going to expand the blockchain paradigm significantly.

Here's a look at the Ethereum application ecosystem as of 2017:

Blockstream

Blockstream is a company working on a variety of projects. The most important of these is increasing the speed of cryptocurrency based projects that work with smart contracts. The company recently saw an influx of more than $50 million during a round of funding. Those funds are being put to work enhancing protocol strength and funding the completion of several projects including the Lightning Network, which will help speed up smaller blockchain transactions and make everyday usage of cryptocurrencies more likely. The Lightning Network received a lot of attention in 2017 as a potential solution to Bitcoin's scaling problems.

Aeternity

Similar to Blockstream, Aeternity is another project attempting to make it easier for Ethereum to grow larger and faster. It is striving to generate a network that would handle all the smart contracts separately from the primary blockchain functions, increasing transaction speeds in the process. The contracts that use this secondary network would only come into contact with the primary blockchain at points where verification of transactions was required.

ContentKid

ContentKid is a unique way of using the blockchain to access streaming content. ContentKid works by purchasing subscription time to various services such as Hulu or Netflix and then renting out the time in short bursts to interested consumers. This allows users legal access to a wide variety of content in daily or even hourly bursts rather than in via a traditional monthly or yearly model. The technology behind it provides users with access as needed by automatically completing transactions based on time spent watching content.

Blockphase

Blockphase is a blockchain based tool that helps combat copyright infringement in augmented reality, 360-degree video, and virtual reality content. Users are able to add their content to the Blockphase blockchain, which then searches the internet for instances of infringement. This allows users to store and manage their copyrights more easily and decreases the likelihood of intellectual theft, freeing them to create as opposed to having to protect their work.

Starting Your Own Cryptocurrency.

Most cryptocurrencies in existence today are clones of the original bitcoin idea, some using the exact same code. As discussed in a previous chapter, each coin has its own separate blockchain, which must be supported by miners, wallets, etc. But what if, instead of creating entirely new blockchain networks for yet more cryptocurrencies, we could use the existing Ethereum platform with its infrastructure already in place?

That is exactly what is happening now.

Numerous currencies... each with their own niches and objectives... have been built upon Ethereum. Depending on the creativity of the developer, these custom currencies can represent a portion of equity in a company, a quantity of a real-life asset, or a portion of profits of a Dapp on the Ethereum blockchain. The possibilities are endless.

Here are some examples:
BitNation (PAT)- A proof-of-concept cyber-government that contains blockchain-based solutions for insurance, education, ID cards, and diplomacy programs like ambassadors, refugees, etc. Bitnation.co
Ethlance - A freelancer platform where workers are paid with Ether. ethlance.com
Swarm City (SWT) - A decentralized P2P sharing economy. Users are required to have a Swarm City Token to do transactions in their ecosystem. Www.swarm.city
Civic (CVC)- Decentralized identity verification via the blockchain. www.civic.com
FunFair (FUN) - a platform for online casinos and gambling. funfair.io
WINGS - a platform for blockchain-based crowdfunding. www.wings.ai

Edgeless (EDG) - another platform for online gambling. edgeless.io

Basic Attention Token (BAT) - blockchain-based digital advertising. basicattentiontoken.org

Metal (MTL) - an end-user digital currency that rewards people for spending it. metalpay.com

Acebusters (NZT) - is a poker platform based on the blockchain. acebusters.com

0x (ZRX) - (pronounced "ZERO-X") a protocol enabling the effortless exchange of Ethereum-based assets. 0xproject.com

1World Online (1WO) - Another advertising platform, this one focusing on interactive media and audience engagement. welcome.1worldonline.com

8 Circuit Studios (8BT) - a gaming platform that uses the blockchain to track ownership of virtual goods. 8circuitstudios.com

HireMatch (HRC) - a blockchain-based employment service. hirematch.io

Kencoin (KCN) - an anonymous currency for transactions related to sex and dating. kencoin.org

Hubii (HBT) - A decentralized content network. www.hubii.network

Storj (SJCX) - a decentralized cloud storage platform. Www.storj.io

This list goes on. Literally. There are over 340 Ethereum-based tokens in various stages of fund-raising, and the list grows daily. Each of these projects and their corresponding tokens have (or will have) a dollar value and will also add value to the Ethereum platform upon which they were built. Any of them could be the next Microsoft, or Steam, or YouTube, or State Farm. However, please note that the legality of some tokens, particularly those involving gambling or ownership of a company, are still murky. Investors in high regulation environments (i.e. the United States) should be wary. *This list is not intended to be a recommendation to buy, sell, or otherwise become involved in anything.*

Future uses

Beyond the projects already underway, Ethereum has the potential to expand into the following areas:

Law

Smart contracts are already making their way into the legal arena in conjunction with traditional contracts. They make it easier to enact all the "legalese" in typical contracts related to the timing and specifics of certain actions. Smart contracts cut through all the red tape and automate things that need to happen once certain external factors are met. In theory, if this practice continues to become more common, there will be less a need for this type of boilerplate content in contracts. It could all be handled automatically in the Ethereum blockchain.

Financial services

The financial service industry is already taking steps to make Ethereum a part of its infrastructure. The Enterprise Ethereum Alliance is racing towards a scenario where the Ethereum platform houses a secondary blockchain tailored to the needs of the financial sectors. Additionally, smart contracts are going to continue to see an increased usage managing trade clearing and the generation of settlements. Smart contracts can also be used to determine coupon payments and in the generation of bonds at the point of expiration.

Smart contracts are also starting to pop up in the settlement of insurance claims. With additional refinement, this type of smart contract would be able to take insurance adjusters out of the system completely. The need for humans would be minimized further as smart cars become able to relay data directly to the insurance company. Insurers would also be able to increase or decrease rates automatically based on predetermined driver statistics. Remember the thought exercise earlier where we removed the humans from an insurance company and called it a DAO? We're only a few years away from that being reality.

Healthcare

Ethereum isn't going to cure cancer, but smart contracts are already helping patients and their data stay connected. Preliminary usage results from hospital testing indicates that linking patients and their charts through a blockchain would decrease the likelihood of clerical errors by as much as 40 percent.

Apps are currently in development that will connect individuals to their health information automatically based on social security numbers. This would mean no more transferring medical records from one doctor to another, or having to track down old x-rays or test results. Everything would be readily available at the press of a button.

The Ethereum platform is also being put to use tracking medical studies. Study participants are having their data transferred automatically for collection. If they are being paid for participation, those payments could happen automatically (via smart contract) when the study comes to an end. Perhaps unsurprisingly, a version of this same technology is on its way to a variety of personal internet devices such as those that track physical activity and fitness goals.

Electric vehicles

Tesla is allegedly working with the Ethereum platform to develop a blockchain-based method of charging electric cars. Owners of electric vehicles would pull up to charging stations and plug in without having to enter payment or identification information. Each car would be linked to a specific smart contract that would, in turn, be linked to a bank account.

Shipping

Work is already being done to put smart contracts to work updating and correlating clerical information. The technology is poised to revolutionize the shipping industry. Supply chain movement will soon be clearly visible in a blockchain that is automatically updated as products move from place to place. Payment will also be handled through the blockchain after products reach a predetermined location. The same process will handle bills of lading, credit and promise payments. As the usage among manufactures grows, the history of every product that you receive will grower longer and more detailed until you are able to track the path everything took from the manufacturer straight to your doorstep.

Chapter 4: How To Buy Ethereum

Disclaimer: I am not a financial or investment adviser. This chapter is general advice only. It has been prepared without taking into account your objectives, financial situation or needs. Before acting on this advice you should consider its appropriateness in regard to your own objectives, financial situation and needs.

We've talked a lot about features, ongoing projects and future use cases, but we have barely mentioned the Ethereum currency, ether. This is intentional. Recall from the introduction that the focus and purpose of Ethereum is its intelligent scripting capabilities... not its currency. Ether is a vital but secondary part of the Ethereum architecture. But that doesn't mean we should ignore it entirely. In fact, given the price behavior over the past year, Ethereum's currency is something that everyone should be paying a lot more attention to.

According to market capitalization, Ethereum is the second largest Cryptocurrency and has the potential overtake Bitcoin. The value of ether has grown at a nearly exponential rate, and it is likely to continue as more ambitious projects built atop the Ethereum platform. in A little ether now could turn into a life-changing amount of money in just a few years... just like Bitcoin.

So how does one actually buy ether?

Creating an account on the exchange

As with any other cryptocurrencies, Ethereum needs to be bought and sold via exchanges. There are many trading platforms. The most popular options include Coinbase (coinbase.com), Gemini (gemini.com), and Bittrex (bittrex.com). Of these three, Coinbase is without a doubt the most newbie-friendly; If you have little or no experience with Bitcoin or Ethereum, I suggest you start there.

Verifying the account

Most exchanges will need to verify your identity before doing much (or any) business with you. New users are frequently required to upload images of identifying documents such as driver's licenses, passports, or utility bills to verify identity and citizenship. After providing documentation, verification can another day or two, depending on how popular the exchange is. Some exchanges won't let you trade at all until you verify your identity while others may limit you to very small amounts. So don't expect to open an account today and buy thousands of dollars in ETH (or any other altcoin). Plan ahead and adjust your expectations.

Depositing currency

If you are trying to buy ETH with dollars (or other fiat currency) the next step would be to deposit that currency into the account. Setting up the connection between the exchange and your bank may be instantaneous... or it may take a few days, depending on the exchange. Once done, it may (or may not) take a day or two for the money to transfer. This entire process may strike some as frustrating and slow... and if it does, recall that this is one of the reasons cryptocurrencies were created in the first place. The roadblocks here are due to the traditional banks and their systems, not with the exchanges.

Speaking of which, you are not limited to buying ETH with dollars. If you already have bitcoin, you can deposit BTC and exchange it for ETH almost instantly (well... in an hour or so). Even better, you can skip creating an account an exchange entirely. How? Use the Coinomi wallet (coinomi.com) on your Android phone or tablet to convert not only between BTC and ETH, but between any of their *many* supported altcoins. Just transfer some BTC into the wallet, use the "exchange" menu option, and select Ethereum as your destination currency. Coinomi uses a service called Shapeshift to execute the exchange. You can use Shapeshift directly (without Coinomi) by going to their website at shapeshift.io. There is not currently an iOS version of the Coinomi wallet, so for Apple fans, the Shapeshift website may be the only option for exchange-less purchases.

Start trading

When your account is verified and money has been deposited, you can start buying or selling ether and other cryptocurrencies. The interface of each exchange is different, and you need to have some patience not only for learning the interface, but for the purchases to be performed once you place the order.

Withdraw the ether into a wallet

Once you have purchased ETH, the next step is to withdraw it into a wallet that is under your control. This is a step that most people... especially new users... skip. They shouldn't. Bitcoin has a long and disturbing history of people getting their BTC stolen from exchanges that were hacked or that turned out to be fraudulent. This isn't implying that cryptocurrency is insecure... but it is implying that cryptocurrency exchanges should not be trusted to store your currency one second longer than it takes to make the exchange. Even popular and trusted exchanges like Coinbase should be used only for converting currency, never for storage. People once regarded MtGox with the same trust they put in Coinbase. They regretted it.

You will need to store your ether in a safe place. Install and use a wallet that supports Ethereum. Wallets are discussed further in the next chapter. For now, recognize and remember the need to use one. Leaving purchases on an exchange should never be your default... this is akin to buying gold jewelry on Amazon and having them store it for you in their warehouse. It takes just a few minutes to find and set up an Ethereum wallet, and if you opted to use Coinomi to make your bitcoin-To-ether exchange, you're already good to go (hint-hint).

Dealing with volatility

It is quite reasonable for markets to suffer price fluctuations, or volatility. Some markets are more volatile than others, particularly commodities and currencies. This is natural. The market for cryptocurrencies is orders of magnitude more volatile than what even experienced investors are comfortable with. High transaction speeds, low transaction costs, and the tendency for the internet to over-react to... well... everything... produces short and medium term price swings that are absolutely awe-inspiring. Dealing with volatility is quite simple. You will just need to get your emotions under control and keep a calm mind. Have a plan and Act. Do not React.

Here is the plan: You should hold Ethereum on a long-term basis. You need to understand that cryptocurrencies... particularly Ethereum... have great potential that hasn't been tapped yet. This potential is what you are investing in. The short and medium-term fluctuations, while they can be frightening and profitable, are largely driven by factors that have nothing to do with that potential. Unless there is a fundamental change in Ethereum that makes it somehow less able to reach its potential... ignore the price volatility and hold. Or, to borrow from Bitcoin terminology: HODL.

Chapter 5: How To Use Ethereum

You will need a secure place for storing your ether and creating transactions. This place is an Ethereum wallet running on a device that you control. The device can be a phone, tablet, desktop computer... or even a piece of paper.

Desktop wallets

The official Ethereum wallet is called Mist, and can be found at https://github.com/ethereum/mist/releases. However, being "official" doesn't necessarily make it better than other options. There are in fact several desktop clients to choose from, and my personal recommendation is not to use any of them. If you're dealing with small amounts of ether, use a mobile wallet instead (see next section). If you're stockpiling investment-level amounts of ether, then skip the desktop entirely and use either a hardware wallet or a paper wallet. Both are discussed below.

Why skip the desktop? There is nothing inherently wrong with any of the available wallets, but most people have a false sense of security when it comes to their own machines. The desktop is a HUGE target for hackers, and yours isn't nearly as secure as you think it is. Most people also use their one desktop for everything from online banking to watching porn. Some of these activities make them even more of a target... and even easier to hack. Unless you have a machine that is devoted to the sole purpose of storing cryptocurrency and is kept offline when not in use... skip the desktop.

Mobile wallets

Mobile wallets run on your phone or tablet. They may not have as many features as a full desktop client, but they are easy to use and definitely newbie friendly. Android has numerous cryptocurrency wallets to choose from. Apple iOS has significantly fewer. Are these wallets any safer than a desktop wallet? Not really. I recommend them over desktop wallets for three reasons. I've already mentioned the first: they are much easier to use. Better user interfaces, fewer advanced features to trip over, and the ability to use a camera to read QR codes make them a clear choice for new users. The second reason is that people tend to think of their desktop as secure and are thus tempted to store large amounts of cryptocurrency on them. Then they go surf the internet, pick up a keylogger or a trojan, and the next time they access their Ethereum wallet, their fortune disappears.

While this sequence of events can happen on a tablet, it is less likely and, more importantly, people aren't tempted to store their life's savings on a cellphone. Finally, people are much more likely to have an old cellphone sitting around than they are a laptop or desktop. Why is this important? That old phone or tablet can easily be converted into dedicated cryptocurrency device that is kept offline when not in use... which will be most of the time.. This makes it almost (but not quite) as good as a hardware wallet.

Hardware wallets

These are small devices that look like fancy USB thumb drives. What they are inside, though, is magic. They have the ability to turn even a known insecure computer into a bulletproof cryptocurrency wallet. All the cryptocurrency operations happen in an encrypted space on the device, invisible to the computer it is plugged into. The two front runners in hardware wallets are Trezor (trezor.io) and Ledger (ledgerwallet.com). Both were originally designed for Bitcoin, but both can be used for Ethereum as well. Hardware wallets cost between $60 and $100 USD, depending on which model you buy and how diligent you are in searching for bargains. This is a lot of money for a device to store pocket change, but if need a place to park thousands of dollars worth of ether, you should strongly consider buying one.

Paper wallets

A paper wallet is a piece of paper (or plastic or metal) with an Ethereum address written on it, along with the code used to access the currency.

We didn't go into the details of how cryptocurrencies work, so it may not be obvious that a Bitcoin or Ethereum address can receive funds even if the wallet that contains the address is offline... but they can. The transactions are stored on the blockchain, not in the wallet. When you open your wallet software, it scans the blockchain for changes to the addresses it controls. Not only that, but if you give your wallet software the secret code (called a "private key") to an Ethereum address that it didn't previously know about, it will then be able to import funds and make transactions with that address. If you combine these two revelations... that addresses can receive funds when not online and that they can be imported to wallets... you have an understanding of how paper wallets work. You can send ether to the address on the paper wallet without fear that its associated computer will be hacked because there is no associated computer. When you need to spend the funds, most wallets will allow you to import the paper wallet address and transfer its contents. This takes only a few seconds and is a lot less complicated than it sounds.

Which Wallet?!

If you've read this far expecting to find a recommendation for an Ethereum wallet, I won't disappoint you. But instead of recommending one wallet for iOS and another for Android and yet another for Windows, I'll give you one name that works everywhere. Jaxx (jaxx.io) produces wallets on multiple platforms that support multiple cryptocurrencies, including Ethereum. It isn't the absolute best wallet, nor is it the one that I personally use, but it is secure and simple enough to recommend to new users.

...and if you absolutely must know what I use for Ethereum: I have a hardware wallet from Ledger and I use the previously mentioned Coinomi wallet on Android. The absolute best cryptocurrency wallet on Android is, in my opinion, Mycelium (wallet.mycelium.com). Unfortunately it does not support Ethereum.

You are the Bank

Regardless of the type of wallet, make sure you remember your passcode and/or wallet recovery phrase. In the case of a paper wallet these are printed on the page which you MUST NEVER LOSE. These passcodes or phrases represent the private keys to your encrypted Ethereum wallet. Losing your private key isn't the same as forgetting the password to your Twitter account. There is no reset. There is no tech support. Without the password, you are permanently locked out of wallet with *zero* chance of recovering your money. If this makes you uneasy... good. That means you're paying attention. Getting rid of banks and other third parties means you are now the bank, and the job of securing your money is 100% yours.

Chapter 6: Ethereum Mining

Note: I include this chapter on mining for completeness, not because I recommend mining as a profitable or fulfilling venture for new users. It isn't. Mining Ethereum for profit isn't something most new users will be able to do without a moderate amount of startup capital, free or cheap electricity, and a high tolerance for frustration. If you are seeking profit, instead consider just buying ETH and holding it as the price rises. If the idea of literally creating money with your computer is too much of an appeal to pass up, then here are the basic concepts.

Mining is the use of computers to perform difficult calculations in a race to decide who gets to write the next block of transactions to the blockchain. The calculations get harder as the number of participants increases. The "winner" gets rewarded in cryptocurrency, and the next race starts immediately after the previous one finishes. That is the shortest explanation of cryptocurrency mining you will ever read.

Solo mining: This when you mine by yourself. The advantage of this is that any mining rewards you obtain are yours to keep. You don't have to share. Unfortunately, mining is difficult, and the likelihood of a solo miner earning a reward is minuscule.

Pool Mining: - With pool mining many miners join forces to try to earn the reward. The resulting currency is then distributed between the minors, usually based on their level of participation. Miners typically pay a small fee to the pool operator for maintaining the service.

Solo miners make money slowly and infrequently. They profit through luck and patience. Pool miners make smaller amounts of money, but they make it more often. They profit by keeping their machines running.

In exchange for mining on the Ethereum platform, miners receive ether to offset their costs and hopefully turn a profit. They also receive a portion of the transaction fees that are charged to users of Ethereum. The value of ether is currently a little over $300, but it changes rapidly... meaning the profitability of ETH mining (measured in USD) fluctuates. A miner may go from making a healthy profit to losing money and then back to profitable again in a matter of days. Worse still, since the mining difficultly is almost always increasing, the machines they use to mine eth become obsolete (I.e. unprofitable) over time.

Getting Started

Finding "the best mining hardware" is a bit like finding "the best computer". It is a rapidly moving target. Hardware manufactures are in a perpetual race to keep up with mining difficulty. Trailing far, far behind both of these things is you and your wallet. The most powerful machine this year may be far out of your price range, and it may also be obsolete next year.

The best place to go for up-to-date information is going to be the Ethereum Mining subreddit at https://www.reddit.com/r/EtherMining/. You should easily be able to find out the current state of the market as well as what hardware is currently considered state of the art. A variety of mining machines can be found on Amazon.com, but that may not be the best place to buy them. Instead of going to a specific retailer and seeing what they have available, find out what you want to buy first, and then search for it on the internet. Don't forget Ebay. Miners will often sell older but still profitable machines to pay for the newer ones.

Regardless of the type of system you choose to go with, you are going to need dedicated hardware in order to mine effectively. While technically you may be able to mine using your computer's video card or your laptop's CPU, specialized mining machines are always going to outpace you. The most popular chips in these machines are made by ASIC and are generally about 100 times faster than a high-end gaming computer. Trying to mine without having the right hardware in place will generally just end up costing you more time and money than the entire endeavor is worth.

Also, remember that these mining rigs... be they overpowered graphics cards or something else... usually need to be connected to a computer and provided with power. Lots of power. Some mining rigs take their power from the computer they're plugged into, which means that computer must have a very strong power supply to support the multiple-mining-rig setups that the pros use. Rigs that have their own power supplies are more expensive, and they still need to be plugged into something to access the internet. This means they may slow down the computer, making it frustrating to use that computer for other tasks. In other words: you might need to buy a new computer or upgrade an old one if you mine at anything other than hobbyist levels.

Getting Online

After you have a mining machine ready, you will need to download the program that you will use to automate the mining process. There are several versions of this type of program available, the most commonly used ones are BFGminer, EasyMiner and CGminer. EasyMiner is the only one that uses a standard graphical interface, the others run via command line prompts. While I don't recommend mining to new cryptocurrency users, EasyMiner is the software they should use if they insist on giving it a shot.

Connecting To a Pool

Once you have the required software and hardware, the next thing you will need to do is to join an ether mining pool. A mining pool is a confederation of miners who band together with the goal of verifying blocks more quickly than they can each do alone. The rewards for doing so are then shared among the miners who helped with the verification. While joining a pool is optional, the amount of computer power required for profitable mining is far what most solo machines can do in a reasonable period.

If you decide to strike out on your own, then you will need to download the Ethereum core client to keep your machine in sync with the Ethereum blockchain. This client can be downloaded from Ethereum.org. Assuming you decide to go with a mining pool instead, then all you will need to do is follow the instructions of the leader of the pool instead.

There are many pools to choose from, each with slightly different rules, fees, and payment schedules. Don't obsess over choosing the perfect one right now. If you're just getting started pick Ethermine (ethermine.org), F2Pool (f2pool.com), or DwarfPool (dwarfpool.com). These are the first, second, and third largest mining pools, respectively. If you can't mine profitably with one of these, picking a smaller pool with different fees won't fix it. Once you know what you're doing, then consider switching pools to earn a fraction of a percent more profit... maybe. Joining up with an extremely popular pool (like the three I listed) means that you will have the chance to get in on more rewards. Going with a smaller pool means that your individual shares from each reward are likely going to be larger. There is a balance point that requires trial-and-error and research to find... but that isn't what you need to be worrying about on your first week mining.

Cloud Mining

It is possible to mine ether using servers hosted on platforms such as AWS (aws.amazon.com) or digitalocean (digitalocean.com). However, this is even less newbie-friendly than buying hardware and the profitability is unproven. Don't waste your time.

There are also Ethereum mining contracts such as those by Genesis Mining (genesis-mining.com). These companies provide you with your own dedicated mining rig hosted in their data center. I advise even experienced people to avoid mining contracts. While Genesis Mining is a reputable company, cloud mining contracts in general tend to be unprofitable. Any profits seen are generally derived from the increase in value of ether, and can be obtained by simply taking the money you would spend on a mining contract and buying ETH on an exchange.

Chapter 7: Three Rules For Cryptocurrency

The moment bitcoin obtained a monetary value, hackers and con-men came out of the woodwork to relieve unsuspecting victims of their BTC. Early adopters navigated a minefield of scams and hacks; every lesson they learned was at the expense of someone losing their bitcoin, often in amounts that would have made them multi-millionaires today. The situation is much better now, but those early lessons still apply, not just to Bitcoin, but to its descendants as well. Fortunately, you don't have to learn those lessons the hard way. Most of the heartache (not to mention bankruptcies) of previous years can be avoided by following my Three Simple Rules for Cryptocurrency.

Avoid web-based wallets. Regard any service that offers to hold your cryptocurrency for you with suspicion. The entire point of Bitcoin (and, by extension, all cryptocurrencies) was to give people direct control of their wealth, eliminating the need for 3rd parties like banks or credit card companies. Using a hosted wallet may sound convenient, but it violates this core principle of cryptocurrency. It is also unnecessary, risky, and not very smart. Using a web wallet is the internet equivalent of giving all the cash in your wallet to a well-dressed stranger who offers to hold it for you. There is no such thing as a "cryptocurrency savings account." There are no "Ethereum banks." Anyone trying to convince you otherwise is suspect. Yes, they may be trying to market a legitimate new, though unnecessary, service. They may also be trying to scam you. You won't be able to tell the difference until it is too late. This rule also applies to online exchanges. As mentioned before, you shouldn't leave currency in an online exchange unless you are intending to trade it in the very near future. The "very near future" is measured in hours, not days or weeks. I cannot emphasize this enough... trusting strangers on the internet to hold money resulted in lost fortunes and ruined lives. I use the Coinbase exchange quite often and recommend that company to new users all the time. I Do Not Trust Them To Hold My Money.

Don't store life-changing amounts of cryptocurrency on a phone, tablet, or computer. Ether, bitcoin, and other cryptocurrencies are incredibly secure. But this security does not extend into whatever computer or mobile device you use. Bitcoin doesn't make your computer hack-proof. Ethereum doesn't make your phone incapable of being stolen. You must understand and appreciate the difference between having a secure application (an Ethereum wallet) and having a secure platform (your phone). Do not store large amounts of currency on insecure platforms. Your desktop, phone, and tablet are inherently insecure and shouldn't be used to store amounts of cryptocurrency that would bankrupt you or cause you to miss mortgage payments if lost. Mobile devices are for "petty cash" amounts... money that you spend in a day or a week. For savings account or investment-level amounts, use specialized secure hardware wallets like Trezor (trezor.io) or Ledger (ledgerwallet.com), or use paper wallets. Remember: With cryptocurrency, you are the bank. Your bank doesn't store your retirement account on a phone, so neither should you.

Don't skip the backups. Most wallets offer a capability to back up your private keys, usually as a string of random words or phrases that you must write down and keep safe. This backup process is simple, but it is awkward and some people choose to ignore it. If your wallet offers a private key backup and doesn't FORCE you to use it... use it anyway. This list of random words is how you will transfer your cryptocurrency to your new wallet if your old one gets damaged or stolen. Think of it this way: suppose you kept your life's savings in a safe inside your house. Now imagine your house catches fire. The password you use to access your wallet is like the combination to the safe. The private key is like a science-fiction teleporter that can transport the safe from your burning house to a brand new one on the other side of town. You might use your passcode every day, but the private key is something you may never need... but if you ever do need it, you will deeply regret not having it. It should go without saying that these backups (usually written on paper) should be kept safe. Keep them in a real, physical safe if you have one. I'm not a fan of storing them a bank's safe deposit box, because you are once again putting a 3rd party in control of your money. But if that doesn't bother you... do it. It's better than leaving your private keys on a notepad beside your computer

Side note: the very idea that you can "back up" your savings and restore it somewhere else via the internet is, in technical terms: Incredibly Awesome.

That's it. You'd think there would be more and, in truth, there is. But the above simple rules represent the biggest mistakes that cryptocurrency users make. They are the answers to questions that new users either ask... or wish they had. Each rule has multiple stories behind it. Very few of those stories have a happy ending. Almost none of them do. Literal fortunes have been lost because people purchased cryptocurrency and were unwilling or unable to take the steps necessary to secure it. As stated before, with cryptocurrency you are the bank. If you cannot do what banks do (hold money securely) then you should keep your cryptocurrency holdings to hobbyist or "petty cash" amounts. I'm assuming that additional guidelines such as "investigate things before you invest in them" and "if something seems too good to be true, it probably is" are obvious and don't need to be stated here, but they apply to cryptocurrency as much, or more, than they do everywhere else.

Conclusion and Further Reading

You've reached the end of Ethereum: A Primer. Thank you for reading.

I've tried to make this book short and interesting, yet still valuable as an introduction to Ethereum. With a topic as complex as cryptocurrency, a certain amount of techno-speak is unavoidable. I've endeavored to keep it to a minimum, but my efforts to do so may have left this book lacking in some of the deeper technical areas. For that reason, I'm going to provide some links to additional resources that you can use to take your understanding of Ethereum to the next level.

But first, let's recap what you've learned already:

What Ethereum Is: A more intelligent and developer friendly version of Bitcoin AND a platform upon which applications can be built.
What Ethereum Is Not: Another end-user currency for buying things on and off the internet.

Why Ethereum is Exciting: It lowers the bar for innovation AND enables much more complex transactions.

You've been introduced to the concepts of **Smart Contracts** (contracts enforced by the Ethereum blockchain rather than by courts and governments) and **Distributed Autonomous Organizations** (blockchain-based corporations with little to no physical presence).

You've seen some exciting projects already underway to bring everything from cloud storage (Storj) to identity verification (Civic) onto the Ethereum blockchain.

You've learned the basic steps for buying and holding ether, the Ethereum currency. You even know to get started mining ether should you chose to do so.

And finally, you've learned my Three Simple Rules for Cryptocurrency, which can be humorously paraphrased as: **Trust No One; Not even Your Computer; Always Have a Backup.** A more serious summary would be **Don't Buy What You Can't Protect.**

Hopefully all of that sounds familiar. If so, then my purpose for writing this book has been met. If you want more, then consider the following links as additional homework:

The Ethereum homepage (ethereum.org) will try to sell you on the features and benefits of Ethereum, but doesn't go out of its way to be friendly to the less technical. Be sure to check out the forum at forum.ethereum.org.

The Ethereum subreddit (reddit.com/r/ethereum/) is an excellent place to keep up to date on Ethereum developments. Like the main website, it assumes a basic level of knowledge that you should already have from this book.

Coindesk's *What Is Ethereum* page (coindesk.com/information/what-is-ethereum/) and Ethereum 101 (ethereum101.org) take everything back down to the basics. If you need a refresher, this is a good one.

On the opposite extreme, the Ethereum White Paper (github.com/ethereum/wiki/wiki/White-Paper) contains all the deeply technical "how's" and "why's" that make most people's eyes gloss over. If you intend to go beyond investing or mining and become a developer or entrepreneur... you should read and understand this paper. Twice.

There is no shortage of cryptocurrency videos on Youtube. Unfortunately, very few of them are specific to Ethereum, and almost none are intended for people brand new to the platform. Nevertheless, Ethereum has an official channel at www.youtube.com/user/ethereumproject. Most of the videos there are technical in nature. Ethereum's creator, Vitalik Buterin, is no stranger to Youtube. Of all biographies, interviews, and technical talks featuring Buterin, my favorite is also one of the most recent: Decentralizing Everything is a TechCrunch interview at bit.ly/TCBUTERIN. There you can watch Buterin explain in his own words what Ethereum is and why it is important. I highly recommend it.

And finally, EthList is a crowd-sourced Ethereum reading list that can take you from "What is Ethereum" to creating your own distributed applications. This list of resources is very long, very comprehensive, and updated often. You can find it at github.com/Scanate/EthList.

These pages, plus the various links they contain, are more than enough to satisfy your thirst for Ethereum. Whether your Ethereum education continues or ends here, I want to say once again:

Thanks For Reading.

Sincerely,
Eric Morse

Cryptocurrency:

A Primer

By

Eric Morse

To the risk-takers, creators, and innovators... and the people that support and encourage them.

Introduction

What is Cryptocurrency?

Magic Internet Money? Digital Currency? Cash for the Internet?
An Incredible Investment Opportunity?

All of the Above.

The word "cryptocurrency" refers to digital "tokens" used to exchange value over the internet. Rather than being controlled by governments or central banks, the values of these currencies are determined solely by the economics of supply and demand. The production and operation of these digital currencies involves encryption, thus the presence of "crypto" in the name. Fortunately, all of the heavy cryptographic math is hidden from the end user by software, allowing users to send and receive money without knowing what a "private key" is.

The definition above, while accurate, is not complete. It doesn't explain why cryptocurrencies were created, what makes them important, or why people use them when there are easier methods for conducting transactions over the internet. It doesn't say why you should care about cryptocurrency. It doesn't tell you which of the hundreds of cryptocurrencies are worth caring about.

Those questions are what this book is for.

Cryptocurrency: A Primer is an entry-level introduction to the world of cryptocurrency. People who are already active in cryptocurrency probably won't find anything new in these pages. The intended audience is who I call the "crypto-curious"... people who have heard of Bitcoin or cryptocurrency and want to know what all the fuss is about. They don't want technical details. They don't want to feel like they're learning a new language or earning a degree in computer science. They may not want to buy or use a cryptocurrency at this point; they just want to know what it is so they can decide for themselves whether it is worth their time. This book is not a step-by-step tutorial or an investment guide. It is an explanation of concepts, and an exploration of history and significance of some of the more important cryptocurrencies. When you reach the end, you will know why people use Bitcoin. You'll know why people are talking about Ethereum. You'll know the story behind DarkCoin. In other words: you'll know what all the fuss is about. Then you can go on to more detailed books on using or investing.

What technical knowledge do you need to bring with you on this trip? Not much. A certain amount of jargon is unavoidable when discussing cryptocurrency, but I try to keep it to a minimum and define new terms where appropriate. It would be helpful if you've at least heard the words "Bitcoin" and "cryptocurrency" before now, and it would be very helpful if you've bought something online at some point in your life. Assuming you paid for this book and read this far into the introduction, you should be okay.

So let's get started!

Chapter 1: Bitcoin (BTC)

Bitcoin is the genesis of all cryptocurrencies and, therefore, has to be the starting point on our journey. In talking about Bitcoin we're going to be discussing concepts which are integral to most, if not all the other major currencies.

Bitcoin is a relatively recent invention born of necessity. Prior to Bitcoin, the primary way of exchanging currency with people over the internet was through trusted third parties such as PayPal, banks, or credit card providers like Visa and MasterCard. In the physical world, the easiest kind of money transfer is to simply hand someone cash; there is no need for a third party. This differs from a bank transfer where you're trusting one or more parties to handle the transaction for you according to terms and conditions agreed upon by... but rarely actually understood by... the account holders.

Bitcoin takes these trusted third parties out of the equation. In 2009, a white paper appeared proposing a brand new currency called Bitcoin based on a new technology known as a "blockchain." The blockchain is essentially a decentralized, public running ledger of all Bitcoin transactions. It replaces the third party in money transfers by authenticating and recording transactions for all to see. The blockchain isn't a bank. It isn't a government or a corporation. It isn't a person, an organization; or single website or server that can be seized or shut down. It is simply a ledger maintained by a network of computers that is distributed across the globe.

Take a moment to think about what this means. The lack of 3rd parties means Bitcoin operates over the internet in a manner similar to cash. Payment processors cannot block your transactions because there are no payment processors. Banks or governments cannot freeze your accounts because you are your own bank.

It's also important that you recognize the utility of the blockchain as a means of recording and verifying information. This information can be anything; it is not limited to account balances and money transfers. Data stored on the blockchain could represent user accounts, deeds to property like houses or cars, marriages, copyrights, licenses... anything. In the specific case of Bitcoin, though, the blockchain is used as a ledger of all money transfers on the Bitcoin network. How one can be certain that the ledger is accurate and reliable? This is where the concept of consensus comes into play. Consensus is the idea of multiple computers verifying the ledger and agreeing which version is the most accurate.

In cryptocurrency, a blockchain is exactly what the name implies: a chain of blocks, each of which contain data. Blocks are connected or "stacked" chronologically. In the specific example of Bitcoin, a single block is composed of many transaction records. When a block is completed and verified by the network, it will be added permanently to the chain. After that, the contents of the block cannot be changed without the majority of the networked computers agreeing to the changes.

Maintaining the blockchain is the job of special nodes on the Bitcoin network, called "miners". Each miner or group (pool) of miners is constantly working on a specific mathematical problem. Not only is this problem difficult, it actually becomes MORE difficult as more people try to solve it. The first to solve the problem correctly gets to write the next block of transactions to the blockchain. In return for their effort, they earn some newly created bitcoin, plus they get to keep all the transaction fees in the block they just wrote. The miner that writes the block gets to pick which transactions get written... and it's in their best interest to pick the transactions that have transaction fees associated with them. Thus, while the transaction fees are technically optional, if you want the miners to care enough about your transaction to confirm it, you should always include the appropriate fee. Most other cryptocurrencies operate similarly, with differences in the exact math problem being solved, how the difficulty scales, how miners are rewarded, etc.

Bitcoin also pioneered the idea of digital wallets, which hold the currency in separate addresses. These addresses are loosely equivalent to banking account numbers. Although this is a vast oversimplification, it is accurate enough for most people to use Bitcoin without detailed knowledge of what is happening behind the scenes in their wallet.

Bitcoin has been a massive success. Since its creation in 2009, its value has skyrocketed from less than $1 to more than $4000 in 2017. It is increasingly accepted as a form of payment by businesses and financial institutions around the world, and some investors see it now as a store of value, much as gold or silver is. But there have been some challenges. Bitcoin - and cryptocurrency in general - is in a gray area legally, Some countries have outlawed it entirely, while others have sharply restricted its use or access to it. The common misconception that Bitcoin is anonymous had led to its adoption by hackers and criminals as a payment method for illicit goods and services. Several major Bitcoin exchanges have been shut down or have gone out of business because of fraud, hacking, or other problems.

Despite these setbacks, Bitcoin and cryptocurrencies in general have grown in popularity. Many users find the decentralized nature of these digital assets very appealing as for the most part they are free from the laws and regulations applied to traditional currencies and financial instruments. But even though Bitcoin is the first and most popular cryptocurrency, it is not necessarily the best. There are many more that have use Bitcoin as a starting point and innovated beyond it. The purpose of this book is to discuss some of these major success stories.

Despite all these newcomers, Bitcoin is still lauded for its history, its consistency, and its trustworthiness. Moreover, it's hard to beat Bitcoin's massive market share; It retains its domination of the cryptocurrency markets.

Bitcoin's official website is bitcoin.org.

Chapter 2: Litecoin (LTC)

The Bitcoin software is open-source. This means that anyone can not only view the source code, but can copy it and make changes to their copy in order to create something brand new. That is exactly how many of the alternative cryptocurrencies, or "altcoins", that are discussed in this book came into being. Litecoin is the first and, at one time, the most popular of these Bitcoin derivatives.

Litecoin takes many of the aspects of Bitcoin but builds upon them. It was first released by Charles Lee, brother to Bobby Lee, the head of BTC China, one of the largest Bitcoin/Litecoin exchanges in China. His intent was to create an improved alternative to Bitcoin. The result was a digital currency some say is the silver to Bitcoin's gold.

Litecoin offered several improvements to the Bitcoin architecture. One major change was the hashing algorithm that was used for verification of transactions on the blockchain. Recall from the previous chapter that writing blocks of transactions to the blockchain is done by special nodes called "miners". These miners are all competing with one another to solve a complex mathematical problem, with a reward going to the first miner (or group of miners) to solve it. In Bitcoin, the math being performed is based on an encryption algorithm called SHA-256. There is no need for end users to know anything about SHA-256, but we need to delve a little deeper than the average user in order to understand why Litecoin exists.

SHA-256 had one big limitation in terms of accessibility and decentralization: it was very easy to dedicate hardware to Bitcoin mining. Shortly after Bitcoin became popular, dedicated Bitcoin mining units... special machines that did nothing but perform SHA-256 calculations... began to appear. These dedicated miners were much more efficient than home computers, even powerful ones, at Bitcoin mining. Soon installations of large numbers of these miners began to concentrate management of the Bitcoin network into a small number of full-time operations, whose sole purpose is the verification of Bitcoin blocks in order to reap the rewards. Recall from the Bitcoin chapter that one of the main features of Bitcoin is its decentralization. Some saw the concentration of mining as a threat so serious that it was worth creating a competing currency to avoid it.

Litecoin tries to prevent this situation by using a different hashing algorithm. This algorithm, called Scrypt, is dependent upon the device's memory and not processor speed. This reduces the necessity to set up massive mining farms and makes mining blocks a more tenable action for the average user.

Litecoin also offered a far faster rate of transaction verification. Where Bitcoin's algorithms solve a block an average of 10 minutes, Litecoin's Scrypt algorithm solves a block every two and a half minutes. This means that transactions are processed much faster than they would be otherwise. In order to make up for this faster block parsing, the Litecoin network produces four times as many currency units as Bitcoin does per block.

Litecoin is interesting in that it has pretty much succeeded flawlessly in its primary goal of being more efficient than Bitcoin. It currently sits in the top five in terms of market capitalization, not far behind Bitcoin and Ethereum. This is perhaps the perfect reflection of what Litecoin set out to achieve. It wasn't aiming to upset the market, but rather to serve as a better version of the major currency. Litecoin didn't innovate on the nature of cryptocurrency, but it did improve on how that nature was implemented. Litecoin is essentially a clone of Bitcoin with different... and arguably better... parameters. Regardless, it sits comfortably with its market cap as the best alternative to Bitcoin for simple money transfers. Litecoin prices have surged from $4 to $80 in the last year.

Litecoin's website is litecoin.com.

Chapter 3: Ethereum (ETH, ETC)

Ethereum is another major form of cryptocurrency. Even though it is one of the most recent, having only been released in 2015, it has become one of the most popular, with the second highest market capitalization after Bitcoin.

Ethereum was first described in 2013 in a technical paper by Vitalik Buterin, a young programmer who played a major part in Bitcoin's early development. His paper proposed that Bitcoin's blockchain needed the capability to allow applications to run on the blockchain. His paper and arguments weren't terribly popular at the time, but they were enough for him to join with several other eager programmers in 2014 to develop a scripting language that gave more freedom and utility to a blockchain.

So, what precisely makes Ethereum different from Bitcoin? The biggest innovation is the implementation of "smart contracts," which provide a way to automate certain agreements or arrangements between two or more parties. They allow the secure and reliable exchange of pretty much anything with a value when certain criteria are met. These criteria are defined by the entities that create the contract. A smart contract is essentially a transaction with intelligence behind it. It is Bitcoin with a brain.

These smart contracts are permanently stored in the blockchain where they cannot be altered without the consent of all the parties involved. This ensures the contract hasn't been tampered with or the terms changed. In addition, the relatively straightforward nature of smart contracts and their implementation eliminates the necessity of a third party or middleman, such as a lawyer or a broker, to guarantee the terms are carried out in full as written in the contract. The smart contract embedded in the blockchain serves as the guarantee. If Bitcoin made payment processors irrelevant, Ethereum did the same for contract lawyers.

Smart contracts run within the Ethereum Virtual Machine, a kind of computer built into the Ethereum blockchain. Each Ethereum node on the network runs the Ethereum Virtual Machine in tandem, providing both security and redundancy. These scripts and smart contracts are typically written in languages like Solidity, Serpent, LLL, or Mutan, all of which specifically geared for the writing of smart contracts. Solidity is the most common and is the primary language utilized by Ethereum; programmers with experience in C and JavaScript will find Solidity to be rather familiar. This offers unparalleled interactivity and potential, which Bitcoin and Litecoin cannot provide, because their code only addresses money transfer and storage.

In two short years, Ethereum has enabled (and inspired) the development of many other blockchain-based projects and has attracted the attention of many traditional financial services institutions. This success hasn't, of course, come without some difficulties. One was large enough to create an alternative

Ethereum ecosystem, which gives us a chance to talk about an important concept in cryptocurrency... forking. This is when a digital asset splits into two different, largely incompatible forms.

One of the first major projects built on the Ethereum network was a venture capital fund referred to as "The DAO." The acronym itself means decentralized autonomous organization, which is essentially a heavily decentralized company running on a blockchain. There can be many DAOs, but in this case we are referring to a specific decentralized autonomous organization, which simply called itself The DAO. If this sounds like science fiction... keep reading; we haven't even gotten to the part about time travel and alternate realities yet.

The DAO comprised the largest bundle of smart contracts to be running on Ethereum and was the earliest, most publicized project on the platform. Its purpose was to collect money from investors and distribute it to projects that the investors voted on... similar to a venture capital firm. The DAO's operation was contained entirely on the Ethereum blockchain. It did not have an address. It didn't have a Board of Directors. It was not incorporated under the laws of any nation or government. It was just a set of rules codified in contracts stored in the blockchain. The DAO was so large, in fact, that it was able to raise roughly 170 million dollars in Ethereum tokens (called Ether or ETH) from investors.

Unfortunately, there were serious security flaws in The DAO's smart contracts, which enabled hackers to steal 3.6 million ETH–roughly $50 million at the time–and move it to different accounts. So much had been invested and stolen that the Ethereum community was vehement about action being taken. There were contentious debates about two options: a soft fork, wherein the pilfered currency would be "burned" or made unusable by either the thieves or the original owners, and a hard fork or a total rollback of the blockchain to a point before the exploit occurred, resulting in a kind of alternate timeline.

A soft fork would maintain the original blockchain in its original form, complete with The DAO's creation and the multi-million-dollar exploit. A hard fork would go back in time and create a new reality where the DAO exploit never happened.

Vitalik and the other Ethereum developers favored a hard fork which was the action eventually taken. However, many Ethereum users disagreed with this decision, as they believed in the concept of the blockchain being immutable and permanent. As a result, they created a version of Ethereum on the unaltered blockchain, which they called Ethereum Classic (ETC). Although the two versions of Ethereum share a common beginning, there are incompatible with each other, rather like humans and chimpanzees have a common ancestor but are entirely different species.

Ethereum Classic is still a major cryptocurrency and, while it lags behind Bitcoin, Ethereum and Litecoin in value, it is still in the top 10 in terms of market capitalization (as of the time of writing), and is also worth your attention.

Despite this early drama, Ethereum remains one of the most technologically innovative forms of cryptocurrency and shows no signs of slowing down. Some day, a cryptocurrency may overtake Bitcoin and Ethereum just might be the one to do it.

Find out more about Ethereum at ethereum.org

Chapter 4: Ripple (XRP)

Ripple is the point of much contention; people either love it or hate it. Ripple is also one of the most poorly understood cryptocurrencies, because it differs in many ways from standard cryptocurrencies like Bitcoin, Litecoin, and Ethereum. Therefore, it's important that we examine the history and intent of Ripple.

Ripple refers to two related concepts: the money-transfer platform called Ripple, and the cryptocurrency, XRP, that used on the platform. The platform Ripple uses XRP as a means of carrying out some of its core functions. Unlike Bitcoin, Litecoin and Ethereum tokens, which are mined over time, Ripple XRP tokens were "pre-mined," meaning that 100 billion were created at the start, and over time will gradually be destroyed or "burned" during transactions.

Ripple has been in development longer than Bitcoin. In 2004 a programmer, Ryan Fugger, developed RipplePay. His idea was to create a decentralized system which would allow new forms of money to be created, functioning through IOUs traded among trusted users. Essentially, RipplePay would keep a log of running value debts, which would "ripple" throughout the network. Somewhat later, the development of Bitcoin in 2009 inspired Arthur Britto and David Schwartz to create a system which would verify the current ledger of transactions not mining, as with Bitcoin, but rather by consensus among users. In 2011 Britto, Schwartz, Jed McCaleb of eDonkey fame, and Fugger formed OpenCoin, which became Ripple Labs two years later.

The intent was to create a system for frictionless money transfers, meaning that transfers would be low cost and nearly instantaneous. Bitcoin had a prohibitively long verification process for point-of-sale transactions, due to the reliance on mining to verify transactions. Verification could sometimes take as long as an hour if the Bitcoin network was especially busy. Mining is also a very power-intensive operation, as the processors use a lot of electricity. Ripple, by contrast, eliminates the need for mining, saving energy and speeding up verification times. Replacing resource-intensive mining with network-wide consensus also reduces the possibility of centralization, which had become a major concern in the implementation of Bitcoin.

This may seem antithetical at first to the concept of cryptocurrency, given that one of the original purposes of Bitcoin was to remove any trust or third party from the equation and allow a simple way for money to be exchanged, but it's actually quite compatible. We'll get to that in just a moment.

OpenCoin (later renamed Ripple Labs) developed the Ripple Transaction Protocol to allow the instantaneous and unobstructed transfer of anything of value, whether it be dollars, euros, yen, or even airline miles, between two parties, and to allow quick and easy currency exchanges across national borders. For currencies with no direct exchange route, XRP would be used as an intermediate currency. The developers then created the Bitcoin Bridge, now one of Ripple's key features. The bridge allowed Ripple users to send any form of currency to a given Bitcoin address; conversion into Bitcoin would happen "on the fly."

Ripple has become one of the top 10 cryptocurrencies, with an $8.36 billion market capitalization at this writing, and has entered into partnerships with an impressive number of banks and other financial institutions.

You can easily see Ripple's appeal. It makes money transfers much cheaper and quicker than existing systems. Prior to Ripple, individuals needing to send money across borders had to use cumbersome third-party services like Western Union or PayPal, or arrange expensive wire transfers through their banks. All of these services charge fees, which can be prohibitive for some users, and in the case of bank wires, the transfer might take days to clear before being deposited in the recipient's bank account. For their part, banks also suffered from slow interbank transfers through existing centralized systems, such as SWIFT.

Ripple replaces these older systems with a peer-to-peer settlement system that was entirely user-focused and that used consensus in order to verify transactions, which would allow an extremely rapid transfer rate. Moreover, Ripple transfers have no built-in restraints, allowing for any currency (or other item of value) to be transferred and exchanged for other any other currency (or item of value) for pennies on the dollar.

So, how does XRP fit into this worldwide money transmittal service?

Unlike Litecoin or Ethereum, for example, the XRP token wasn't intended to compete against or improve upon Bitcoin. In fact, the two complement one another, as the Ripple protocol allows the easy exchange of any form of currency including Bitcoin. Instead, XRP was developed as a compliment to the Ripple protocol, and as a means by which the parent company could generate capital. Half of the total supply of XRP is retained by Ripple Labs and will never be in circulation. [Note: At this writing, 1 XRP = $0.21, so the XRP held represents more than $900 million.]

While holders of XRP have to maintain a minimum balance of 30 XRP in their wallets in order to use the system, XRP in most cases is not even necessary for the Ripple platform to operate. The Ripple network relies on trusted gateways for transfers. If two gateways can use euros for cross-border transactions, for example, they don't have to send XRP to make the transfer. XRP is used only for the very low transfer fees. In this sense, Ripple is quite different from Bitcoin, Litecoin or Ethereum.

Ripple may be the first major cryptocurrency to make an impact on the global scale with banking, but it's not the only one. We'll talk a bit later on about NXT's Mijin blockchain and how it has the potential to change banking's internal infrastructure, as Ripple has begun to change banking's external infrastructure with fast, cross-border transactions.

You can find Ripple's official website at ripple.com.

Chapter 5: Storj (STORJ, SJCX)

Most cryptocurrencies exist for a specific reason. Bitcoin was intended (among other things) to eliminate the reliance on 3rd parties for monetary transactions. Litecoin was meant to be a faster, more centralization-resistant version of Bitcoin. Ethereum was a smarter Bitcoin. Storj is unique in that its purpose is extremely specific AND totally unrelated to monetary transactions. Like Ripple, it is not a clone of Bitcoin, but is something totally new.

Storj aims to take a really fundamental and common idea and turn it on its head. Storj, in the company's own words, is a "platform, cryptocurrency, and suite of decentralized applications that allows you to store data in a secure and decentralized manner." In other words, Storj takes something that is already decentralized... cloud computing... and takes it several steps further. Instead of having data stored on a central server, as with Google Drive or Dropbox, it is instead stored on a peer-to-peer network of computers. Files are first encrypted so that no one but the end user of the files can access or open the data. Since the data is decentralized and distributed across the network, losing access to one's files is highly unlikely as you are not depending on a single point of storage. In other words, Storj is to cloud storage companies what Bitcoin is to payment processors and banks.

But where does all of this storage capacity come from, and what does any of this have to do with cryptocurrency?

Anyone can participate in the Storj network by sharing part of their unused hard drive space in exchange for money. Originally these participants were paid in SJCX, a Counterparty-based cryptocurrency. Counterparty will be discussed in a later chapter. Payments for using the network to store files were also made in SJCX, and sales of the SJCX altcoin were used to raise money for the project. Recently, Storj transitioned from SJCX to an Ethereum-based altcoin called STORJ. Payments are currently accepted in US Dollars and BTC.

The STORJ project isn't particularly interested in competing with Bitcoin or Ethereum. After all, neither Bitcoin nor Ethereum offer cloud storage. The project's developers introduced their own token so that they could use it for their own personal reasons, as well as to give the company a financial kickstart from sales of the tokens. (This kind of Initial Coin Offering, also called an "ICO", has become a very popular crowdfunding vehicle.) Moreover, the developers wanted to ensure the platform's flexibility and stability with a custom-made currency, instead of relying on an external currency over which they had no control.

In that sense, STORJ isn't a particularly fascinating investment. Storj as a service is likely to grow gradually, at least in the short term, so you probably will not see rapid exponential growth as happened with Bitcoin and Ethereum. Rather, the value of STORJ tokens will rise slowly over time, as the service gains market share. Storj is important for several reasons. First, Storj is·a project and business built on cryptocurrency who's purpose is largely unrelated to currency or monetary transactions. It is an evolution of purpose; it represents the next layer of development... the use of cryptocurrency technology as a platform rather than as a product in and of itself. Storj also represents a return to early days of Bitcoin when the average user could participate meaningfully in the network and be profitably reimbursed for their efforts. Bitcoin mining has been far out of the reach of the average user for some time, and even most altcoins require better-than-average computers in order to keep up. With Storj, however, a spare hard drive is all one needs to help the network and earn money doing so.

Learn more about Storj at storj.io.

Chapter 6: DarkCoin/DASH (DASH)

One cryptocurrency about which there is a large amount of contention is Dash, which has one of the highest market caps of any digital asset. Dash started out as just another cryptocurrency in a time where the Internet was being flooded with Bitcoin clones. However, Dash set out to be a little bit better than the competition.

The key problem that Dash was attempting to solve was lack of anonymity in transactions. Bitcoin proponents have often claimed that Bitcoin is anonymous, but it isn't. Bitcoin is pseudonymous. When Bitcoin transfers are made, they are stored in the blockchain as a record of which party made a transaction to whom, at what time and of how much. The parties involved are identified by their Bitcoin addresses, not by names, social security numbers, or any other personally identifiable information. The Bitcoin addresses are pseudonyms, in that sense. Since the entire blockchain is a public record, it is possible to deduce who owns those Bitcoin addresses by following chains of transactions until you reach one where one of the parties reveals their identity, either intentionally or accidentally. With sufficient effort, names can be attached to addresses, and the illusion of anonymity disappears.

In other words, Bitcoin transactions are not inherently anonymous and can be traced back to the end user. However, it is possible to further hide the real-world identities of Bitcoin users by "mixing" Bitcoin transactions, so that the association between address and user is obscured. The best analogy for mixing is this: Let's say that you've got a dryer with a bunch of identical shirts tumbling around in it. You can put a shirt in and take a different shirt out. You won't know whose shirt you have pulled out, and nobody is going to know if they pulled yours out. Since your shirt has just been tumbling around with a bunch of other shirts, there's no way to prove that any given shirt is yours.

While there were (and still are) mixing services available for Bitcoin users, mixing is not an inherent feature of the Bitcoin platform. Dash changed that. Mixing is built into the Dash client and is intended to provide security and anonymity in all transactions. Used in conjunction with a proxy service or the TOR network, it would be possible for Dash transactions to be completely untraceable.

Despite the obvious advantages Dash offers, many critics are apprehensive about Dash and some even go so far as to call it a scam. To understand why, you have to understand its history.

Dash was first released in the very beginning of 2014 under the name XCoin. It was released two days earlier than advertised, during which 1.9 million coins were pre-mined, or brought into existence outside of the mining process that creates new bitcoin and Bitcoin-like currencies like Litecoin.

This is one big point of contention that leads some people to believe Dash is a scam.

Mining ahead of a project launch and starting out with a set number of coins is known in the cryptocurrency community as an "insta-mine." This insta-mine, in particular, was purportedly accidental, but insta-mines are heavily frowned upon because a small number of people could end up with a majority of coins before the public has a chance to buy them. Hypothetically, these early holders could manipulate the value of the coins and profit unfairly from trading the coins on the open market. In the stock market world, this would be known as insider trading, which is illegal. This kind of pre-mining is what soured some cryptocurrency purists on Ripple/XRP, which launched with all the available tokens already available, and significant amount in the hands of the developers.

The cryptocurrency community is split on whether the XCoin insta-mine was truly an accident. The story given by the lead developer, Evan Duffield, is that it was the result of a bug in the source code. Looking at the history of the source code, one can see where Duffield tried multiple times to make changes to the code in order to save the currency and stop the insta-mine. It took several tries before he was successful, and by that time, nearly ten percent of Dash's estimated maximum coin count had been mined.

Duffield attempted to salvage the situation by offering to relaunch the coin. The XCoin community, however, vehemently disagreed with this idea and it was abandoned. Duffield then suggested the possibility of giving coins away in order to broaden the distribution of the coin. Yet again, the community disagreed. At this point, it was decided: XCoin would be left alone to develop as it would.

A month after the launch, XCoin was renamed as DarkCoin. And in 2015, it was renamed yet again as Dash, an abbreviation of "Digital Cash."

Is Dash is better than Bitcoin? Each currency has its advantages. Bitcoin certainly has a larger market share and acceptance as it benefits from being the first cryptocurrency. But Dash comes loaded with many features that aren't present in Bitcoin, such as instant transactions and the aforementioned anonymity capabilities.

The truth is that Dash was gunning hard to become the "Bitcoin" of the future, but its shaky start may have doomed it to contentious obscurity. To counteract the bad publicity, the Dash team has made special public relations efforts to promote the currency, and improved the Dash wallet's user interface to make it easier to use. Dash has a market cap as of this writing of $2.4 billion, but it has lost momentum and is no longer in the top 10. With almost half of the cryptocurrency community being distrustful of it, it's not in a good position to be used by online vendors where other cryptocurrencies, such as Bitcoin, Litecoin or Ethereum, are used more freely. This attitude may change, however, with the Dash team's PR campaigns.

Dash's official website is dash.org.

Chapter 7: NXT

NXT is one of the most groundbreaking cryptocurrencies available. NXT was first proposed as a "second generation cryptocurrency" by an anonymous coder in 2013. Unlike many other popular cryptocurrencies, NXT was not built upon the codebase provided by Bitcoin or Ethereum, but rather was built from the ground up using Java. As such, it was able to diverge in some ways from other cryptocurrencies while retaining some similarities.

The central idea was for NXT to take core ideas and concepts from Bitcoin and Ethereum and build upon them, offering a full-fledged blockchain platform that can be used to do almost anything. One major difference between NXT and Bitcoin is the token supply. Bitcoins are constantly being created through proof-of-work (mining). In the NXT ecosystem, however, there is a static supply of money, which means that new coins aren't created by mining. Rather, transactions are verified through proof of stake, or one's ownership of NXT tokens. In fact, NXT can be seen as a proof of concept for the "proof of stake" idea, as 100% proof-of-stake blockchains were previously thought to be unworkable.

Relying on proof-of-stake also means that anyone can verify a block using any device, even something as simple as a Raspberry Pi or a smartphone. There is no such thing as specialized "NXT mining" hardware, and even small players still have a chance to verify a block and receive a reward.

Proof of stake is also innately more efficient than proof of work consensus algorithms, meaning that transactions will happen faster than they would with Bitcoin or even Litecoin.

Another key idea was to create a platform that could implement many important different blockchain features within one blockchain. Because of this, NXT isn't just a cryptocurrency for money transfers; it also offers a suite of services, including additional currencies, an asset exchange for share trading, data storage, a messaging system, an alias registration system, and even a voting module useful for any context, be it political or business. It also has a wide array of support for different plugins, which allows users to easily add their own features to the NXT client and create new applications.

Perhaps the most impressive thing that the NXT system is its support for new monetary systems. The currencies created are backed by the NXT coin itself, but are independent of it. The anonymous founder of NXT, BCNext, said that it was best not to consider the cryptocurrency, NXT, as the most important currency of the system, but rather as the foundation for brand new currencies.

Basically, NXT coin and Bitcoin serve different purposes. NXT coin isn't supposed to be a major feature in and of itself, but rather serve as part of an even bigger platform. Meanwhile, the Bitcoin blockchain was invented primarily for the purpose of establishing a workable digital currency. Meanwhile, the NXT and Ethereum platforms both allow for the creation of new currencies and services on top of their blockchains.

When all is said and done, NXT's intent was to create a next-generation cryptocurrency. In that respect, it has succeeded and NXT is now in the top 20 cryptocurrencies by market capitalization. While NXT is not as famous or as widely used as Bitcoin and Ethereum, it is an innovative cryptocurrency worth keeping an eye on.

Learn more about NXT at nxtplatform.org.

Chapter 8: Other Cryptocurrencies of Note

As of this writing there are over 800 distinct cryptocurrencies, with new Initial Coin Offerings appearing almost weekly. It may be impossible for any compendium of cryptocurrencies to be all-inclusive, but there are certainly those deserving at least a mention even if they do not rate a full chapter. This chapter lists other cryptocurrencies worthy of mention either due to historical significance, ambition, innovation, or just plain quirkiness.

ZCash (ZEC)

Zcash is yet another cryptocurrency with a major focus on anonymity. Similar to Bitcoin, it has a fixed maximum of twenty-one million coins, but its mining algorithm was designed to give home-based miners with ordinary computers a chance to mine, making the process more democratic and decentralized than Bitcoin mining. In this sense, it is a combination of Dash and Litecoin.

Zcash was introduced by Zooko Wilcox-Ohearn in September 2016, with the intent of building upon the work of cryptography researchers from multiple universities, especially Johns Hopkins. The researchers had been working on a privacy protocol known as Zerocoin since 2014. Zcash was the logical outcome of that research.

The specific ways in which Zcash implements privacy are rather robust and a bit difficult to explain. Basically, Zcash utilizes zero-knowledge proofs in order to disguise the identity of the sender and the recipient, as well as the overall amount of the transaction. Explaining zero-knowledge proofs is beyond the scope of this book, but the end result is that anonymity is created by making the sending and receiving address any random address on the blockchain itself, similar to the mixing principle discussed earlier. Zcash, like Dash, also gives the users the option of using publicly viewable addresses, if they desire.

Zcash has in one year become a very important cryptocurrency. It has resided comfortably in the top 20 cryptocurrencies indexed by market capitalization. It fulfills a similar purpose to Monero (discussed later) in offering real anonymity in your private transactions, despite a public blockchain.

Zcash's website is z.cash

Dogecoin (DOGE)

For many people, their first and most amusing foray into altcoins was the *Dogecoin*. The Dogecoin (or "DOGE") is based around an Internet meme which superimposes misspelled Comic Sans text over a smiling Shiba Inu dog. While Dogecoin was originally a joke; the initial programmer wanted to create a cryptocurrency that would reach more people than Bitcoin by being fun and lighthearted. Additionally, the development of Dogecoin was an attempt to purify the image of Bitcoin, which had become associated with darknet marketplaces, such as the Silk Road and Alphabay, which sold illegal drugs, pornography and other illegal goods and services.

Dogecoin uses the Scrypt algorithm, as does Litecoin, which makes it difficult to create dedicated mining devices, enabling anyone to mine Doge. Dogecoin has a much shorter block time than Litecoin does, which means blocks are verified faster. Additionally, it offers a different mining block difficulty algorithm from Litecoin's, which is specifically intended to discourage mining pools.

Dogecoin was officially released in December of 2013 and jumped sharply in value in the first 3 days. After this brief popularity surge, the value dropped by 80% after many enthusiasts started to take advantage of the ease of mining the young coin.

Dogecoin is mostly now used as a way to tip people online. But the Dogecoin community and the Dogecoin Foundation have become a major fundraising force. Dogecoin campaigns have sent a bobsled team to the Winter Olympics and have established wells in Kenya in a campaign called Doge4Water.

Dogecoin's official website is dogecoin.com. There, you will find what is undoubtedly the catchiest and most memorable intro-videos of any cryptocurrency.

Primecoin (XPM)

Primecoin is particularly interesting because of its proof-of-work system. Instead of spending processing power on a difficult but otherwise meaningless encryption problem, Primecoin miners search for chains of prime numbers. This system results in some key differences between Primecoin and Bitcoin.

The first is that within Primecoin, the amount of the currency at any given time, and thereby the scarcity of said currency, is largely defined by the distribution of different prime chains. Therefore, the coins dispensed aren't held back rigidly by pre-defined algorithms, but rather by the natural distribution of a certain numerical property. Likewise, there is no limit to the amount of coins available as there is with Bitcoin. Transactions are confirmed approximately ten times faster than with Bitcoin. In addition, the difficulty level of Primecoin mining is adjusted very slightly after every block.

Primecoin is not likely to catch on as a major cryptocurrency or compete toe-to-toe with Bitcoin or Ethereum, but it's an impressive work of coding that does an amazing job of showcasing a unique and useful concept.

Learn more about Primecoin at primecoin.io.

Namecoin (NMC)

When it comes to interesting and unique, but relatively unknown cryptocurrencies, it's difficult to beat Namecoin. It was released in April 2011 as the first project to branch off from Bitcoin. The intent of Namecoin was to allow the development of an alternative domain name service (DNS), which registers and keeps track of domain names on the

Internet. Traditionally, this has been kept under centralized control by ICANN, or the Internet Corporation for Assigned Names and Numbers. The intent of Namecoin was to create a DNS which would be free from any sort of censorship and free from ICANN's control. In other words, Namecoin was developed as a means of protecting and, in some manner, *enforcing* free speech. Every domain name established by way of Namecoin ends with the *.bit* extension, which serves the same purpose as the more familiar *.com* or *.net* domains.

As cryptocurrencies, Bitcoin and Namecoin have almost no differences. For example, both will cap at 21 million individual units. Namecoin and Bitcoin are so similar that they actually share the same cryptographic techniques, allowing enterprising miners to swap between the two depending upon which is more profitable at any given moment.

Beyond the initial purpose of establishing an alternate decentralized domain name system, Namecoin can also be used as a means to set up blockchain support for things such as messaging and even voting. The system is built with versatility in mind and aims to provide as many possibilities as it can insofar as they pertain to Namecoin's particular niche.

Learn more about Namecoin at namecoin.org.

NEM(XEM) and Mijin

NEM is a cryptocurrency and blockchain platform, which at first was intended as a fork of NXT, but instead was built from the ground up. It offers many of the same services as NXT, but its architecture is significantly different. An associated technology, Mijin, is a private blockchain designed specifically for the banking sector.

NEM uses a new method of block verification known as proof of importance or PoI. It is designed to be even less resource-intensive than proof of stake algorithms, which NXT uses, and a lot less than proof of work algorithms, which Bitcoin uses. Like NXT, PoI can run on pretty much any machine, even a Raspberry Pi. The nature of the algorithm also encourages people to use their tokens rather than just keeping them waiting for the value to appreciate. NEM has a dedicated mobile wallet to encourage using NEM's token (designated as XEM) for everyday purchases.

NEM is designed to be more secure and much faster than Bitcoin. Developers are also working on incorporating smart contracts, such as Ethereum offers, into the NEM system. Additionally, NEM is the first major crypto platform to provide support for private blockchain development.

That's where Mijin comes in. It is a private blockchain offering faster transaction times and major improvements in efficiency. Like Ripple, Mijin represents one of the first cryptocurrency technologies to be considered by the mainstream financial industry and, moreover, suggests the possible acceptance of cryptocurrencies as a form of exchange equal to physical fiat currency.

Nem's website is nem.io, and information on Mijin can be found at mijin.io.

IOTA (MIOTA)

IOTA completely rewrites the concept of the blockchain. Whereas the typical blockchain has a linked chain of unique blocks, each storing different, but sequential information, the IOTA system depends on a *tangle* architecture. In a tangle, any given block will point to the two blocks prior to it, creating a super strong and secure data collection. This allows an infinitely scaling system of transactions. Moreover, since there are no blocks, there are no transaction costs. The last major boon that IOTA provides is the potential for transactions to occur outside of the context of the world wide web. IOTA hopes to leverage the "Internet of Things" (IoT) into the tangle.

IOTA could be a major driving force to allow Internet-enabled household appliances to communicate with one another, both to process transactions on the tangle and to make the end user's life easier. As IOTA is still in the process of being fully developed, it may be premature to delve into its details just now, but the technology shows great promise.

IOTA's website is iota.org.

Monero

Monero, like Dash, is intended to offer more anonymity than Bitcoin, but may in fact be more effective at it than Dash is. Originally developed as a fork of the cryptocurrency Bytecoin, it launched in April 2014 as *BitMonero*, taking the word *bit* and combining it with the Esperanto word for *coin,* "monero". Bytecoin, which still exists as a minor player in the crypto world, was a privacy-focused fork of Bitcoin.

Monero comes chock full of numerous privacy features. First, ring signatures are used to hide the wallet address of the person sending Monero, which means that the sending wallet cannot be tracked. Next, a new technology, RingCT or Ring Confidential Transactions, will hide specific information pertaining to the transaction, such as the amount transferred. Lastly, the receiving address is also obfuscated. These privacy features have helped Monero to jump into the top 10 cryptocurrencies by market capitalization, with a $1.7 billion market cap.

Find out more about Monero at getmonero.org.

Stratis (STRAT)

Stratis has only just recently debuted, but it has already reached a market capitalization of half a billion dollars. That's quite impressive for a newcomer to the cryptocurrency world. Stratis has become popular for two reasons. First, the Stratis development platform offers allows decentralized applications to be created within the platform, meaning that coders have a whole new set of tools to experiment with blockchains and cryptocurrencies. Perhaps more impressive, Stratis gives private organizations the ability to establish their own blockchains, which can then integrate with these new applications as well as the main Stratis blockchain. This offers an easy entry into the world of blockchains to anyone interested in experimenting with it.

Learn more about Stratis at stratisplatform.com.

Counterparty (XCP)

Counterparty isn't a cryptocurrency in and of itself. It does have a token, XCP, that can be bought, sold, or traded, but this capability is actually a byproduct of Counterparty's true purpose. Counterparty is a Bitcoin-based platform where new coins and other assets can be created on top of the Bitcoin blockchain. They are not Bitcoins themselves, but they use the same transaction process. They can also be used in conjunction with standard Bitcoin addresses, which simplifies accounting for the end users. Despite these shared resources, one's Counterparty and Bitcoin wallet balances exist independently of one another.

At the height of its popularity there were dozens, if not hundreds, of Counteryparty-based tokens. There were tokens representing video game assets, IOU's for digital and physical goods, voting rights in businesses and organizations, access to members-only portions of websites, and so on.

The predecessor to STORJ, SCJX, which was discussed earlier, was originally built on the Counterparty platform. A lesser known example of a Counterparty-created currency is LTBcoin, which was introduced by the hosts of the popular Bitcoin podcast, Let's Talk Bitcoin. They use the currency as a means of thanking those who help them in one way or another with the podcast. Using LTBcoin gives the user a substantial discount for podcast services as well as at various online stores that LTB has partnered with. It can also be used for tipping. It's a good example of a cryptocurrency intended only for a specific set of users.

Counterparty's official website is counterparty.io.

Zcoin (XZC)

Zcoin is a new cryptocurrency with a history that only stretches back to September of 2016. Like many others, Zcoin is an attempt to bring enhanced privacy to the cryptocurrency sphere. It is an implementation of the Zerocoin protocol created by professor Matthew Green of Johns Hopkins university in 2014. Zerocoin technology was originally intended to be added in Bitcoin, but was instead implemented as a separate coin, Zcoin, by Poramin Insom in 2016.

Unlike other attempts at anonymity which rely on obscuring transactions by mixing them with other transactions, units of the Zcoin currency are created on demand with no previous transaction history, and then destroyed after being used. Zcoin's operation requires lots of complex encryption, but the end result is a cryptocurrency that cannot be traced. Its objective may be shared by many other currencies in this book, but its approach is novel. Zcoin is worth keeping an eye on.

Zcoin's website is zcoin.io.

Ark (ARK)

ARK is a self-described "sandbox of blockchains" that seeks to be a network and platform upon which other cryptocurrencies are built. Ark uses smartbridges to connect to other blockchain-based currencies like Bitcoin and Ethereum, giving users the ability to transfer value among altcoins with a simple transaction. It has a number of as-yet undeveloped features on the development roadmap, including a dropbox-like file system, smart card integration, and enhanced privacy via the use of bridges to other blockchains. More importantly, the Ark team comprises a number of well-known crypto-developers devoted to bringing the features to life. While Ark's eventual feature set seems mostly targeted toward developers, Ark's intent is to become a very consumer-friendly end-user currency. Ark wants to attract developers with features and ease of development on their platform. Developers will, in turn, create blockchains with features that end users actually want (such as enhanced privacy). These blockchains will all be interconnected by Ark via the smartbridges.

Ark was launched in March of 2017. More information is available on their website at ark.io.

Chapter 9: Investing

It is impossible to discuss cryptocurrency without someone bringing up the topic of investing. The questions are universal: Should I invest? How much? Is now a good time, or should I wait? Have I missed the boat on investing altogether? Which currencies are worth buying? Where and how do I buy them?

Normally I sidestep these questions by pointing out that an introductory text is not the proper place to seek investment guidance. I usually follow that up with my standard advice that:
1) You shouldn't invest in things you do not understand, and
2) You shouldn't invest money in cryptocurrency that you can't afford to lose.

Most people aren't satisfied with that advice. People are making hundreds, thousands, and millions of dollars trading cryptocurrency, so it's only natural to be curious on the topic, even if you don't actually plan on investing at all. So, to the crypto-curious who what to know what I think, I will offer my opinion here.

But first, a disclaimer:

Disclaimer: I am not a financial or investment adviser. This chapter is general advice only. It has been prepared without taking into account your objectives, financial situation or needs. Before acting on this advice you should consider its appropriateness in regard to your own objectives, financial situation and needs.

Now that that's out of the way, let's talk.

The currencies listed in this book were chosen because I either found them interesting, innovative or thought they had historical significance. "Interesting" and "innovative" do not necessarily equate to having a future of ten- or hundred-fold increases in value. "Historical significance" could easily mean that a particular currency's race has already been run. In short: you shouldn't take an altcoin's presence in this (or any) book as a recommendation to buy.

However, of the coins discussed here, there are definitely some that I would recommend to an investor who's financial objectives and risk tolerances were similar to mine. If I were given a sum of money and told to buy some of the currencies in this book, here are the ones I would absolutely buy:

Bitcoin: Bitcoin is an elder statesman; a blue-chip stock of cryptocurrency. I think there is still a lot of upward potential and consider any price less than $10,000 a bargain. This is only a 2X to 3X increase in value from its current levels, so, while there is money to be made, it probably won't be the life-changing windfall that people want it to be.

Ethereum: The DAO debacle, the associated hard-fork, and my own skepticism kept me out of Ethereum until recently. That was a mistake. Once I dug deeper and saw the real capabilities of this platform, I realized that, early stumbles aside, it is better than Bitcoin with even more upside potential.

These two currencies would make up the bulk of my portfolio. These are my "Buy and Forget" investments. I expect both of these coins to be around and trending upward for a very long time. I have confidence enough to ignore short term pull-backs or fluctuations in value, assuming they weren't caused by some change in the fundamentals of the currency. If China decides they want to ban Bitcoin again and the price tanks, I'd use that as a chance to acquire some cheap bitcoin. That is the smart move. However, if the Bitcoin developers decide to remove the 21 million BTC cap on the number of coins, I'd jump ship, as this fundamentally changes what makes Bitcoin valuable.

Once I had taken an appropriate position in Bitcoin and Ethereum, I would diversify into one or more of the privacy-focused altcoins, such as Zcoin, Zcash, or Monero. Privacy has always been a cornerstone of cryptocurrency, and I've seen it become even more of a buzzword lately. Notice that I didn't include DASH here. I don't think DASH is a bad altcoin, but its baggage is holding it back. I'd rather back one of the newcomers. Right now, I'm rather fond of Zcoin. In the end, however, I think only a few of the privacy-focused coins will be successful. They may all continue to exist and have value, but I don't believe there is room for more than one "mainstream privacy coin". I don't know which altcoin that will be, so this is not a "buy and forget" type of investment. This is more of a "buy low and hold while watching for signals" investment. This effort, while minimal, may be more than most people are willing to undertake. That's understandable. Not everyone wants to be a trader, and not everyone wants to spend an hour reading about cryptocurrency every day. Those people should stick with Bitcoin and Ethereum.

Finally, there are several coins that I might not buy right now, but I would definitely want to learn some more about. They might be worth taking a position in... or they might not. But they are worth looking at. These coins are IOTA and ARK. Each of these has ambitions to bring needed features to areas undeserved or ignored by cryptocurrency. They are not alone in these ambitions... but they have shown more marketing and/or development effort than most of their competitors.

You can purchase most of the currencies in this book at Bittrex (https://bittrex.com). Exchanges are usually made between Bitcoin or Ethereum and the currency in question. I do not use Bittrex to purchase Bitcoin itself; instead, I use Coinbase (www.coinbase.com). I am not affiliated with either of these companies except as a customer. My willingness to mention them here is based on my personal experience, not on any investigation or examination performed by me or anyone else. You should NEVER leave cryptocurrency on an exchange after making a purchase. Always... ALWAYS... transfer your currency to a wallet that you control. Exchanges like Bittrex and Coinbase are for buying cyprotocurrency, not storing or using cryptocurrency. Bitcoin's history is full of examples of what happens when people ignore this advice. Don't be an example, and don't say you weren't warned.

This concludes the investing chapter of a book that probably shouldn't have an investing chapter. Go back and read the warnings and disclaimers that you skipped over on your way here. People who are brand new to cryptocurrency... I.e., the target audience of this book... shouldn't be putting their money into it. Don't invest in anything you don't understand. Don't invest money in digital currencies that you can't afford to lose. If you are going to invest in cryptocurrencies, make sure that you carefully research the topic and the specific assets you wish to buy. Cryptocurrency markets are very volatile, and there are few guarantees that a particular asset will survive more than a few years after its launch. Wise investments, however, can be quite profitable, as recent history has proven.

Further Research

Thank you for reading *Cryptocurrency: A Primer*.

This book was intended to provide a basic level of education on cryptocurrency. It is not an exhaustive exploration of all the available cryptocurrencies, a technical treatise on how blockchains work, or a guide to using them securely. This book's target audience is new users, and most new users don't need that level of detail at the start. However, if you've gotten this far you've graduated from the level of mere "crypto-curiosity," and are now ready to learn some of those details.

So where do you go from here?

I've included links to the official websites of each of the currencies I've discussed. Some of those pages, especially those of the lesser-known altcoins, are filled with marketing hype or technical jargon that you might not be ready for. Most, however, have videos that have simple explanations of the altcoin's features. If you're after technical information, search the websites for links to whitepapers. Most cryptocurrencies have one, and reading it is a bare minimum for anyone wanting to invest.

If you want more detailed but still newbie-friendly information on Bitcoin, I suggest my collection, *Using Bitcoin,* which combines three entry-level books that cover everything from mining to setting up a wallet. Each of the books in the collection is also available separately. Visit my Amazon Author page at bit.ly/EricMorse for my complete catalog. I will be publishing a book on Ethereum later this year. Join my mailing list at bit.ly/EricMorseList to keep abreast of new releases.

Youtube can be a goldmine of information on all aspects of cryptographies. Unfortunately, you'll need to wade through a lot of misinformation, hype, and sales pitches to find anything useful. Rather than overwhelming you with an exhaustive list of videos and channels, I'm only going to recommend two people. The first is Andreas Antonopolos. You can find his channel at https://www.youtube.com/user/aantonop. Andreas has been speaking to end users, developers, bankers, and politicians for years about cryptocurrency. He does an excellent job of tailoring his talks to the level of his audience, and he is one of the smartest men in crypto. Any video with this name and face on it is worth watching. My second recommendation is a relatively new channel called DataDash run by Nicholas Merten. The channel's URL is rather unwieldy, so I've used a shortener to make it easier: http://bit.ly/data-dash. Nicholas focuses on the investing side of cryptocurrency. He has videos examining and introducing new altcoins, and also has very detailed lessons on trend analysis and market signals. I don't agree with all of his recommendations, but I will say without reservation that if you want to be a cryptocurrency investor, DataDash is where you should start. Between Andreas and Nicholas, you have access to enough information to make you an expert.

Thanks again for reading. May your cryptocurrency journey be interesting and profitable.

Made in the USA
Las Vegas, NV
09 June 2021